Teacher, You Look Like A Horse!

Lessons From The Classroom

Also by Frances H. Kakugawa

Wordsworth the Poet
Mosaic Moon: Caregiving Through Poetry
The Path of Butterflies
Golden Spike
White Ginger Blossom
Sand Grains

Teacher, You Look Like A Horse!

Lessons From The Classroom

By Frances H. Kakugawa

WATERMARK
PUBLISHING

To all the children, in and out of the classroom,
who became the best of my teachers —
and to that little kindergartner who told me
I looked like a horse.

© 2003 by Frances H. Kakugawa

All rights reserved. No part of this book may
be reproduced in any form or by any electronic
or mechanical means, including information
retrieval systems, without prior written permission
from the publisher, except for brief passages
quoted in reviews.

Library of Congress Control Number: 2003109407

ISBN: 0-9720932-9-X

Cover Photography by Lew Harrington
Design by Leo Gonzalez

Watermark Publishing
1000 Bishop Street, Suite 806
Honolulu, Hawai'i 96813
Telephone: 1-808-587-7766
Toll-free 1-866-900-BOOK
e-mail: sales@watermarkpublishing.net
Web site: www.bookshawaii.net

Part of the proceeds of this book are donated to
the HSN Foundation for the promotion of academic excellence in the schools.

With special appreciation to Maya Angelou for
permission to use an excerpt from *Wouldn't Take
Nothing For My Journey Now*, Random House,
Inc., copyright 1993 by Maya Angelou.

Special appreciation also to Howard Gardner of
the Harvard Graduate School of Education,
author of *Frames of Mind* and *Multiple
Intelligences,* for allowing me the poetic license
to use his name.

Printed in the United States of America

CONTENTS

ACKNOWLEDGMENTS

Thank you to George Engebretson and Duane Kurisu of Watermark Publishing, for having faith that this book can make a difference in students' lives. A special word of gratitude to George for his creative vision and his trust in my words.

To Ted Plaister, my first editor, for wholeheartedly supporting the content of *Teacher, You Look Like A Horse!* before red-penning the rough drafts.

To my former students Jennifer Hee, Ryan Hirasuna, Howard Magner, Destiny St. Laurent, Trebor Struble, Teresa Ainsworth Todd and Robert Webster, for saying yes when asked to write the last chapter for me.

To the children and adults who have come into my life and become my mentors, including those whose names I changed here to protect their privacy. Thank you for allowing your stories to be told.

Frances H. Kakugawa
Honolulu, Hawai'i

Introduction

This is a book about teaching. It's as simple as that, or as complicated. Clearly each teacher's odyssey is different, but because I have experienced such great joy and so many rewards from teaching and working with children, I thought my own journey might be of interest and help to teachers — those just starting out or those who have traveled the teaching road for some time — and to parents or anyone else with the privilege of being in the presence of children.

As I left his College of Education class at the University of Hawaiʻi for the last time, Dr. Robert Clopton said to me: "If I pass your classroom someday and there is absolute silence, it'll mean one of two things — your children are all dead or your classroom is empty. And if you really want to hurt and insult me, you will say this when you meet me on the street, 'I *had* the History and Philosophy of Education from you.'" It was his way of pointing out that learning is an ongoing process.

On my first day as a sixth-grade teacher, an experienced colleague advised, "Do not smile for a whole month and you will have total control." A teaching partner told me, "If you want good evaluations, walk your students in a straight line around the principal like robots and soldiers, and he will leave you alone. Do this now and then."

My teaching life began simply and innocently in a kindergarten class. That day, a child brought in a copy of LIFE magazine's *Book on Astronomy* to class for share-and-tell time. Knowing the text of this book was too difficult for five-year-olds, I proceeded to show them the illustrations without reading from the book, supplying instead my own comments. One child piped up, "Why don't you read the book?" Another quickly explained, "The teacher young yet. She don't know how to read."

That child was partly right. I was young and so I reacted with the pride and righteousness of youth. I rebelliously thought, *I don't know how to read, eh?* I began reading the book, word for word, and in no time at all the children's attention had vanished. All the while I thought I had proven my point — that the text was too difficult for them — thereby establishing myself as the wise and all-knowing teacher.

Many years have passed since that first class, and my own youth is a matter of history. The truth, which I learned bit by bit over the years, is that teaching is not a simple and innocent matter. Yes, I am a bit wiser but I have not reached that state of all-knowing in terms of how to teach, and probably I never will.

Over these many years of teaching, the memories of certain children who graced my classrooms have been permanently etched in my memory. With this book, I wish to bring them forth once more so you can meet them, listen to them, ponder what is said, and learn from them as much as I did. These children refused to be dead, or to let me teach in an empty classroom. They demanded that — to meet their needs — I become a lifelong learner myself. These are the children who brought a smile to my face from the first day, and who walked in a rather crooked line. These amazing children took me far beyond all curricula, learning theories and the totality of educational research to what I consider to be the heart of education.

My wish for you is that you not only enjoy reading about these children but, best of all, come to the realization that if you will let it happen, "by the children you'll be taught." This invitation is extended to all adults who are in the presence of children of all ages. ●

I | RED NAIL POLISH

My decision to become a teacher was based on the only other alternative I thought was available at the time — becoming a prostitute. Perhaps I'd better explain.

Kapoho, which lies buried under lava today on the Big Island of Hawai'i, was my birthplace and childhood home. This little village had no electricity, no water system and no telephones except for three party-line telephones located in three of the four grocery stores. There was one generator-powered movie theater and tiny Kapoho School, a three-room facility taught by three teachers, none of whom had a college education. The eruption of the volcano in 1955 and later in 1960 buried everything we owned: our kerosene lamps and stoves, kerosene-run refrigerators, gas irons, water tanks, outhouses, and our battery-run radio which had brought to this isolated place such programs as *Arthur Godfrey, The Romance of Helen Trent, Young Dr. Malone* and *The Lone Ranger*.

Remote, yes, as we were separated from the much larger town of Hilo by an hour's ride on an unpaved country road, but we were not deprived of the wiles of the world. The word prostitute was as household a chunk of language to us as were Christmas and the Easter Bunny.

As we played barefoot on the dusty roads, we watched in awe at the common sight of sleek black cars, driven by well-suited men and filled with tall, high-heeled, heavily made-up women, entering the Filipino camps. We may not have known exactly what they did but from the whispers, we knew it was something dark and forbidden. The high heels seemed almost stilt-like as the women fought to keep their balance while walking through the gravel on the road after leaving their cars.

It was during this time in my life that I developed a strong liaison between the world of the prostitutes and myself. Their red nail polish symbolized for me a bit of elegance, a touch of New York City, something that was out-of-Kapoho. But red nail polish was associated with prostitutes, and therefore, girls with painted nails were whispered to be both wild and immoral. These, too, were the girls who had "soldier babies" during the war.

One day, after a visit to the dentist in Hilo, I secretly purchased a bottle of red nail polish at the local Kress Store. I painted one pinky red, thinking surely one little painted pinky wouldn't be so evil and bad. But a maiden aunt told me that this was worse than 10 painted fingernails. Didn't I know that prostitutes usually kept one nail longer than the others, painted red, a sure sign of her trade? Thus red nail polish became forbidden fruit for me.

In September of one of my high school years at Pāhoa School, I met the typing teacher, which was a turning point in my life. It was not my favorite, "Thanatopsis," that I memorized out of sheer pleasure or the frogs I had dissected in science class that helped to decide my future. Rather, it was the typing teacher whose every nail was painted red. Imagine being a teacher so respected and dignified, she would be allowed to wear bright red nail polish!

Every morning, after getting off the bus, I stood on the second floor of the school to watch all the teachers walk from their cottages to the office. What a parade of sophistication and dignity they presented: dresses, stockings and red nail polish. I knew then that I, too, would someday become one of them.

I did, in time, become one of them but it took two scholarships and a live-in maid's job to reach that dream. At 18, my own maturity had taken me far beyond my childhood and high school perceptions but nevertheless, I have strived to live my life in as many dignified ways as I could.

Not everyone is cut out to teach, and it is, in fact, unfortunate that there are teachers who have no business being in the classroom. When I began my student teaching, I was asked to write why I wanted to become a teacher. To one of my sentences, "Needless to say, I enjoy children," the supervisor noted, "This needs to be said. This is very important because not all teachers enjoy children."

I understood my supervisor's comments with clarity later when I received the following comments from my own student teachers to the question: Why did you select a teaching career?

> *To find a mate in the teaching field.*
> *I couldn't decide on a career so decided on teaching.*
> *Because I'll have my summers off.*
> *My parents want me to be a teacher.*
> *My mother's a teacher, so I thought I'd be one, too.*

Perhaps these teachers are cut of the same cloth as those who advised me to not smile the first month of school, to treat my students like robots and to keep them in line at all times. Perhaps these are the teachers whose classrooms are silent and empty.

When teachers ask, "Where do I begin to become a better teacher?" my response has always been, "Begin with yourself." A teacher takes all of herself into the classroom and who she is becomes her classroom and the basis for her relationship with her students. For example, a person who can't be wrong will not listen except to her own voice. A person who has a strong critical parent inside of her will find all the wrongs and will be blind to the little rights in her students. A person who is not a life long learner will teach from out dated theories and concepts and turn a blind eye to new research findings. A person who explores herself will turn her classroom into one of exploration of new ventures and a safe place for learning. Clearly, the more psychologically and emotionally well-adjusted a person is, the healthier her classroom will be.

Teachers would be well advised to read not only the professional literature, but also those books that speak of self-development and growth.

?

If I could have
But one symbol
For my quest
For transformation,
It would be
Merely this…
?

Step One

So many paths,
So many quests.
Where do I begin?
I'm up to my chin
In all this din.

There's Trust and Respect
Or is it Values and Facts?
Inquiry and Reflection,
Responsibility and Collaboration.
Prior Knowledge with the New.
Self-direction and Experience, too.
Time, Relevance, Practices,
And etcetera, etcetera, etcetera.

So many paths,
So many quests.
Where do I begin?
Where do I begin?

Begin your journey
With one simple step…
With what it is to be human.

Frances H. Kakugawa

The teacher wields almost total power in the classroom. Nowhere is there a place where one adult can have so much control over young children and teenagers. Only in the classroom do we find the situation where students need permission to use the bathroom. I have always felt most uncomfortable to be given so much power in the classroom. To ease my own discomfort, it was important for me to explain to my students that "the only reason you need my permission to use the bathroom is because I need to know your whereabouts. This is my responsibility as your teacher, to always know where you are." Students seem to appreciate this approach to the subject of bathroom privileges and made me feel less powerful in an otherwise over-controlled environment.

"What! You get paid for teaching us?" This question from third-grader Ryan caused me to look at my red-painted nails. I understood his incredulous look. He was really asking me, "What? You're not here because you love being with us? You're here because they pay you to be here?" Momentarily, I was tempted to stretch the truth somewhat and say, "No, I don't get paid."

During one of the teachers' strikes, my sixth-grade class told me they didn't want to know how much I was getting paid. They remarked, "Not much, right?" They wanted assurance that I was there because I wanted to be with them and not for the money.

One day, however, I blew my cover. I had taken some empty shoeboxes to class. Students love these boxes to store their supplies and personal secrets. I heard a commotion in the back of the room over all my shoeboxes. One student said, "Look at this! This costs $59.99!" "That's nothing," another said. "Mine says $69.99!" They were comparing the price tags on my shoeboxes. They couldn't believe a poor teacher would be able to afford such expensive shoes. They looked at me and asked, "Are you rich?" meaning, "Have you become rich because of your teaching?"

"No," I weakly lied. "Those shoes were all on sale. Real good sale."

I had proven the claim that I'd made to my student teaching supervisor: "I enjoy children." The enjoyment of children must also maintain that line of separation between teacher and students. Only then will there be the respect and dignity we require in our classrooms. That very thin line of professionalism that separates teacher from student needs to be cultivated from Day One so students know "You love us, you like us, we are friends but we can't abuse this relationship. You are still our teacher and we will not cross that line out of respect for you." It is apparent students understand this relationship when they apologize to me on the playground when they inevitably use language not appropriate to the classroom. Or when they test the relationship and stop in mid-sentence or mid-behavior and say, "Sorry." As I explore certain aspects of my experiences in the classroom, the word "magic" comes to mind. Perhaps "magic" explains how certain relationships happen in the classroom.

Many former students who remain in contact over the years find it difficult to address me by my first name with but a few exceptions. For example, the week Howard Magner graduated from college in Oklahoma, he called and sheepishly asked, "Now that I'm a full-fledged adult, may I ask you some questions?" I said he could and he then asked me some questions pertaining to my personal life, all of which I answered. What Howard was doing was establishing a new relationship between us, one that erased some of the old boundaries. I love the "Dearest Frances" greetings I continue to receive from him. I find it interesting we have not met face-to-face since his sixth-grade year with me, yet he remains in touch with me. And, it took him the time from the sixth grade until his graduation from college to finally muster enough courage to seek permission to "cross the line."

The teachers' lounge offers endless opportunities for self-evaluation and the acquisition of new knowledge from fellow teachers by listening carefully to what is said. These gatherings point out with considerable clarity the differences among teachers. For example, some teachers enter the lounge with a glow on their faces, unable to contain their most recent and precious encounters with their students. They speak of one student's Ah, Ha! in learning, or their own version of the breakthrough phenomenon in their teaching. On the other hand, there are those who come into the lounge day after day, expressing their discontent with what goes on in the class-room, blaming those "damn kids" for whatever failures occur. My response to those teachers who damn their children is simply to paint my nails a brighter red so as to remind myself of the dignity, honor and privilege of being a teacher — and that I must never abuse these tenets required of those in the teaching profession. 🍎

2 | TAKE TEN

Teachers who go to their schools during the late summer months to duplicate their year's work for their students in all subject areas have always amazed me — in an uncomfortable way. What is it that they know and have that I don't? Is it ESP perhaps to know each of their students and their learning styles and interests even before meeting and getting to know them? These are often the same teachers whose second career consists of attending teacher workshops to collect lesson and unit plans written by other teachers for other students.

First-grade teacher Helen Bowman of Maui spends her late summer months with her students instead of the copier. She meets with each student and their parents in order to gather as much information as possible about each child. On the first day of school, she knows their interests, fears, strengths and weaknesses. She knows what each child looks like before printing up their first day of school nametags. With this crucial information in mind, she begins each school year.

Howard Gardner, author of *Frames of Mind,* speaks of the multiple intelligences of people; yet, all too often, many seize upon one holy way of teaching in the classroom — the paper and pencil, fill-in-the-blanks method. If we would involve the students in the teaching and learning process, we would only require blank sheets of paper and pencils instead of mounds of duplicate worksheets. Or perhaps, not even a single sheet of paper but rather a wide-open mind filled with ongoing knowledge of what our students are like as individuals and of how learning best takes place.

The ready availability of that duplicating machine has done more damage than good to the learning process. How do I best teach? What is the simplest and easiest way for me to teach? I have asked myself these questions repeatedly during my first few years of teaching. Fortunately, my questions evolved into "How do students best learn?" Moreover, I discovered that how I best taught wasn't necessarily the best way students learned.

There would not be Oscars and Golden Globe Awards if all filmmakers were satisfied with Take One and said, "Cut! Print!" It takes good directorship and writing to bring script and actors together on screen. It takes actual filming to see what works and what doesn't work.

If we teachers were in the film industry, we would fail miserably with the attitude of, "I had my script, I did my directing, but the actors did a poor job. Oh well. I'll go on to the next scene or film."

Yet in the classroom we often settle on Take One and think nothing of it. What have we ignored and adversely affected but the students' love and spirit for learning?

Just as a good script does not guarantee an Oscar-winning film, a good lesson plan does not guarantee successful learning. Rather, it is the involved and interested interaction between our students and the lesson plans that makes for good learning, with the students taking lead.

Change in educational practices takes courage and risks. It takes a healthy person to say, "I need to step out of this comfort zone of current teaching ways and look at myself critically as a teacher."

I often cringe in regret when I think back to some of my practices in the classroom and how long it took me to adopt new paradigms. I took my students from reading basal books to whole language learning concepts. In retrospect, in the late '50s and early '60s there wasn't a broad base of good research on how we learn. The textbook publishers were pretty much calling the shots on what and how to teach and they had their own agendas that, sadly, often were not driven by student outcomes but rather by financial gain. In short, book companies dictated what was best for our classrooms. This is not nearly as true today because of the volumes of educational research available, influencing what is published in curricular resources.

Yes, my first graders did learn to read using the original basal readers, but there were many casualties, too. During my teaching career, I retained two students because they were not up to grade level as specified by these reading programs.

There were other casualties, including students who were beyond the levels specified in these basal readers. However, I was not trained to do anything but to fit these students into the curriculum. During my third year of teaching, Jason came to first grade knowing how to read. I hated this because I didn't know how to accommodate him in a classroom of more than 30 students. He just didn't fit in with the rest of the class. What was I to do? This is cringe time in retrospect. Jason read from the beginning readers without complaint. But I feel now that I insulted him and wasted his time in my class.

How better to show you some near casualties than with two of my students and friends? "Hey, Gardner" is a poem written to capture my observations in middle and high school classrooms. Joey, in whose voice I wrote "I Learned to Read in the Parking Lot," is a personal friend of mine.

Hey, Gardner

Man, things are sure different around here now.
Same teacher, same class
But something's not the same.
Hey, don't get me wrong,
I'm not complaining, not yet anyway.
But is it my imagination
That the teacher's more interested
In me?
Before, all I needed to make it in here
Was paper, pen and my body
For attendance count.
These past weeks, I noticed
The teacher being more interested
In what I'm saying or doing.
She even lets us move our chairs and desks around.
Lot of talking by us, too. Not only by the teach.
Before she used to get on my back
Because I was always scribbling cartoons.
(Yeah, I have a few on her)
Paper and pencil, that was the order of the day.
Me, I'm no writer.
I have all these ideas in my head
Like anyone else but
Tell me to write them out
And they all freeze right there.
But hey, give me a drawing pencil
Or a paintbrush
And all these ideas in my head
Flow out into my brush
Like there's a lifeline

Between my brain and my brush.
So what's different now?
I noticed my teacher listening more
To what I say. She asks me a lot of questions,
Not those education-type questions —
You know — like the ones straight from the book?
But she asks me how I spend my spare time
Outside of school.
Hey, last week she even gave us a choice.
"If you could have a choice,
How would you work in here?"
Me, I'm always testing her out
So I threw my pen into the wastebasket,
Like a Celtic, and said, "Not with that!"
Hey, she looked actually happy
As though I had passed her test.
I expected a "Pick that up!"
But instead she asked kind of quiet-like,
What would you use?
"A brush," I said, "Or this."
I took out my drawing pencil
That I hide inside my desk
For those boring times, you know,
Which is all day ... until now.

So what's happening today?
I'm doing my research project in cartoons.
You ought to see my friend Zac.
He's actually writing a song.
This is Zac, who used to spend half the time
Down at North Shore.
He even brings his guitar to school now.

The girls, as always, are in a group
Writing and putting on a play,
Except for Kelly
Who likes to figure things out by herself
So she's working alone.
This quiet kid whose name I'm not sure of
Told me once he doesn't like to think.
He's building something with toothpicks.
Another strange thing ...
There are a lot of adults in here now ...
The teacher has invited these musicians,
Artists, writers, into our class to help us out.

You know what?
I look at all the different ways
Kids are doing their stuff in here
And I have this weird idea
Like hey ... maybe the teacher
Had a brain transplant.
Maybe she got a brain
Like one big puzzle with lots of puzzle pieces,
Instead of that gray brain mass
Found in our physiology book.
And each of these pieces reach out to us.
The music piece reaching out to kids
Who like to work with music,
The language piece reaching out to kids
Who like to write,
And of course that piece called art
Reaching out to me.
Well, whatever, this is better
Than what it was before ... I think ...

And I'm sticking around.
Who knows, maybe someday
I'll even pick up my pen again.
Or even learn some music from Zac.
Hey, Gardner. Thanks.
I think.

Frances H. Kakugawa

I Learned to Read in the Parking Lot

My name is Joey. I'm in the first grade ... again. My teacher told my mommy I couldn't read so I had to stay in the first grade again. But I can read but my teacher doesn't know this.

My friends from last year all tease me during recess. They say, "Look at Joey. He's in first grade again this year. He's not too smart." I try not to hear them because I don't want to be called dumb. I wish I were home instead.

My mommy and daddy don't think I'm dumb. In fact, they're always saying how smart I am. Especially my Dad.

One day I saw a pretty blue car so I asked my Daddy, "What's that car, Dad?" He said, "That's a Camaro. Do you know how to spell Camaro? C-a-m-a-r-o." I liked that, so I asked my Dad to spell it again. C-a-m-a-r-o. "Hey, Dad, I can spell it, too. C-a-m-a-r-o. My Dad put his hand on me and said, "Wow, Joey. You're good." That made me feel good, so I never forgot how to spell Camaro. After that, I began asking Dad about all the cars I saw on the streets. Now I can tell the names of all the cars and I can even spell them: Continental, Volkswagen, Oldsmobile, Datsun, Toyota. Everything.

So Dad takes me riding all the time so I can spell all the names of the cars. Once I wanted to see what a Volvo was like so

Dad took me to the car dealer and now I can spell *Volvo*. Sometimes he takes me to the car lot and we have fun as I find the cars and spell the names for my dad. Every time I spell a car's name, my dad lets me spell it for my mommy when I go home. My aunts and uncles ask me to spell , too. They keep saying how special and smart I am.

On my birthday they all bought me a lot of model cars. Even an Oldsmobile, Cutlass and Mustang. I now have a big collection of cars. And I can read and spell them all.

But at school, the teacher doesn't ask me to spell or read the names of cars. She gives me a book and asks me to read. The words look strange and when she tells me the words, I get scared and can't remember. My hands get all wet and cold. The other children say, "But that's such an easy word." But it's not easy for me. *Volkswagen* is easy for me.

The teacher keeps me in at recess to help me. It's funny. I can read at home because I'm not scared. In fact, I'm always reading at home. My mom leaves mayonnaise and jelly jars on the table for dinner all the time. She doesn't put them in a dish. It's more fun this way because I'm always saying, "Hey, Dad, I know what that says. 'Keep in cool place.'" He tells me, "That's right, Joey. You're good." Why do I feel dumb in school? Why can't I read in school?

One day my mom gave me a box of Jell-O and said, "Joey, think you can read this and make dessert for dinner?" Wow. She wanted me to make dessert. So I read the directions on the box and she helped me with the measuring cup. My dad said that was the best Jell-O he ever ate. Now my mom lets me help her make other kinds of desserts all the time. Too bad I can't make Jell-O in school. Wouldn't my teacher be surprised if she knew I could read Jell-O boxes?

My dad and mom are always reading and they let me look in their magazines. One day I saw a Volare in their Time magazine. "Hey, Mom. Can I cut out this Volare?" "Sure, Joey, after we get through with the magazine." Now I have a big scrapbook with all the cars in it. My mom helped me write the names of the cars under each one. I can read the whole book without help from anyone.

One day my mom had to take me to the doctor because the teacher said I had to be checked by a doctor. The doctor asked me all kinds of questions. I liked him a lot so I told him, "I can spell and read cars." He asked me if I knew how to spell Pinto. I spelled it for him. He called his nurse and asked me to spell Pinto for her. She got excited and they both said I was smart. Now whenever I go to see the doctor, he has a new car for me to spell. I like him.

My dad likes me, too. One day I asked him, "How many telephone poles on this street, Dad?" Know what he did after work? He took me walking to count the telephone poles. The next day I wanted to know how many poles there were on the other streets so he took me walking again.

Every day, as soon as he came home from work, he took me walking. We counted telephone poles and electric poles. He told me how the men have to climb those poles to fix the wires. He told me how we get electricity. My dad's smart. And he tells me I'm smart.

The other children still tease me at school and say I don't know how to read. My teacher lets me do more coloring than the other children. And when the other children are reading books, she lets me play with puzzles by myself. I don't like school.

During recess one day, my sister in the sixth grade was mad at her classmate because he told her she had a dumb brother. So my sister told him, "Can you spell Continental? Because Joey can." He didn't believe her so he called me and said, "OK, Joey, spell Continental." I spelled it. He said, "Spell Rolls Royce." I spelled it. He said, "Wow." Then he called his other friends and told them I could spell all the hard cars. They asked me to spell more and I spelled them all. I know my sister was proud of me because she came closer and closer to me. After that, they didn't call me dumb at recess.

The next day, the principal took my hand and said, "Joey, come with me." He took me to the parking lot and let me name and *spell all the cars in the lot. He acted just like my dad. He called me smart and put his arm around me. I wasn't scared. The next day he took me to the parking lot again. It was fun. I felt good.*

The next day my teacher let me find pictures of cars in magazines and she let me cut them out. I wrote the names of cars on the paper. She put my work on the board. I didn't feel dumb anymore. The other children stopped to look at my cars, too.

One day the teacher took the book out again. It was funny. This time I wasn't scared. I knew how to read some of the words in the book because I have been reading them at home. When I didn't know a word, the teacher helped me. And I could remember them now. Sometimes I even read new words by myself. Just like magic. I still read all the words on the bottles and cans in the supermarket because it's fun. I still like to look for cars. But I can read in school, too. And no one calls me dumb anymore.

Me

I can hardly be seen
Among the mountains and the clouds.
Just a tiny speck, obscure and small.
Yet I exist. I exist.

Frances H. Kakugawa

Teaching is very much like that infamous road to Hāna, Maui. It is not a straight and narrow drive but one rife with curves, blind spots, dips and bumps. At times it is best to take a rest along the roadside to catch your breath and settle your stomach. Or maybe turn around and take a helicopter instead, depending on the circumstances of that particular day. Such it is with teaching. We need to begin our journey each morning with an open mind, flexible plans and joyful anticipation of where we're heading. And with some laughter thrown in for good measure, for without pure enjoyment, what's the sense of being alive?

Happily, sometimes, our best-laid plans go astray and we need to Take Ten. And if all the gods are with us, we may even need to just Take One. This was not to be with *Charlotte's Web*.

I began reading *Charlotte's Web* to my class of third graders. After the second day, I began to see copies of *Charlotte's Web* in the students' hands. Books were being borrowed out of the libraries, both school and public and parents were purchasing paperbacks for their children.

As the story progressed, I saw more children following the story with their eyes. Every day someone would remind me, "You're on page so-and-so." When the book was completed, other children began borrowing *Charlotte's Web* from children who had the book and they began reading the book over again. In the meantime, I began discussion toward an activity I had in mind: to make a mural of all the major characters in the story and to see the changes that had occurred in each. Our discussion left me open-mouthed:

"Wilbur had to make a decision about death. Wilbur found out that death isn't the end. The babies are part of Charlotte so Wilbur will always have Charlotte," said Hallie.

"Wilbur was like a baby at the beginning and cared only for himself but at the end, he cared for Charlotte," said Steve.

"Wilbur couldn't make decisions at the beginning but at the end he decided to take Charlotte's egg sac home," said Kristina.

"Templeton never changed. He still had to be bribed," added Jon.

"Fern became interested in boys," said Nick.

I didn't expect phrases like "decision about death,"

"death isn't the end" or the insights they had to offer. I was delighted as I could see these on the mural.

After a few days, our painted mural was completed except for the description of each character change. In the middle, there was the barn. Around the barn, like a web, were Charlotte, Wilbur, Templeton and Fern. Between the characters were parts of the setting and other secondary characters.

One afternoon, because we had 15 minutes before dismissal time, I read poems to the children, carefully selecting poems with clear metaphors and images. I suggested the children work with such metaphors and images in their spare time. Brie wrote the following poem:

Charlotte's Web

A tear rolls down Wilbur's face.
"Charlotte, don't die.
I'll be heartbroken if you do.
You're my best friend,
You saved my life
By writing words in your web.
You made a miracle.
You made people believe
That I was some pig,
Radiant, Terrific and Humble.
Come back, Charlotte!"
Sadly I get into the crate
And leave my Charlotte behind.

I looked at the mural and at Brie's poem and my plans for a character-change mural died a fast death. I put her poem between Wilbur and Charlotte.

Wendy, who had silently proclaimed herself the poet laureate of our class, was absent on these days. When she returned, I saw her go to the mural to read Brie's poem without a comment. I thought, "Yes, Wendy, write a poem." The next day Wendy's poem was put between Fern and Wilbur:

The Runt

His adoring eyes look up at me.
He's the runt.
Through his silky white ears
The sun shows.
He's the runt.
I love his cute and tiny smile.
He's the runt.
Nobody ever cares for the runt.
He never wins medals or prizes.
Does it really matter
That pigs come in different sizes?
Everyone thinks he's an outcast.
That is, everyone but me.

Then Hallie said, "Someone should write about Templeton."

"Hallie," I asked, "Why don't you?" I put her poem on the mural near Templeton:

Templeton

The luscious food:
Rotten apples,
Soft tomatoes.
Rotten eggs,

Soggy hot dogs.
Stick lollipops,
Wet cotton candy.
Smashed bread,
Sticky gum.

The delightful garbage cans,
The gooshy banana peel.
People running rapidly by.
It's over.
All over.
All mine.

Other students came to ask, "Can I write a poem about something else?" Up went another bulletin board with the heading, I AM A POET. Take Ten. ●

3 | I KNOW SOMETHING I CAN'T TELL

The older one's students are, the more open, honest and up-front a teacher needs to be with them. With younger children, I found practicing fairness without verbal explanations to be sufficient because they are still in the pureness of their childhood where they know they can trust me as their teacher. The older and more sophisticated they become, the more my approach to this fairness game has to take a different turn.

On the first day of school, when we all begin our work at establishing rules and classroom procedures, I found it useful to include the following:

As your teacher, I have information about each of you which the rest of you don't know about. Because of this information, there will be times when I will not be able to treat you equally and I will sometimes appear to have a teacher's pet. I won't be able to be fair all of the time. For example, if there are students experiencing divorce in their family and are in great pain, I will do anything possible to help them and I may need to ignore some classroom rules. If ever you find this difficult to deal with, come and see me and we will talk.

A class of sixth graders taught me it takes courage to not play fair the year Angela entered our classroom. I heard her before seeing her. It was the morning of the second day of school in September. As I sat at my desk going through my class list of sixth graders I suddenly heard a lot of chatter and movement in the back of the room. My first impression was, "Oh, oh, here comes trouble."

She was an attractive girl of 12 with dark eyes, who twisted and turned in all directions, watching the students who were beginning to settle down in their chairs. She was laughing, talking and moving her arms all at the same time. I thought of a caged animal suddenly set free and knew she'd be a handful because most students enter a classroom very cautiously and apprehensively on their first day of school.

She had entered the classroom through the exit door. Her name was Angela. After a few days of school, Angela began to reveal her academic inadequacies. She could read at the beginning of first-grade level and her writing looked like a first grader's in June. I thought of Pigpen in the Peanuts comic strip because wherever she stood, there would be a ring of students around her or a cloud of emotions encircling her. Her face could burst into the juiciest smile or contrarily be turned into the darkest and most turbulent sea. I knew I had to proceed gently with her as I saw so much distrust in her eyes as they constantly flitted from one person to another, as though she was constantly on her guard.

It was a full-time task keeping Angela in her chair as she could generate interest and disrupt the class with just a silent look. Being essentially a non-reader, she could not do any of the work her classmates did. There would be sudden bursts of laughter and a long line of teasing words in the midst of a lesson as she tried to get attention from the boys. Her "OK, OK," to me didn't last very long. The rest of the students of average or above abilities chose to ignore her by quietly observing from the sidelines.

There were two behaviors Angela knew I wanted from her: to come to class on time and to go directly to her desk. After I spoke with her about not observing these two behaviors, I would find notes like the following on my desk, which had been illustrated by someone else. This note included a smiling Snoopy.

Dear Miss Kakugawa
I am sorry From being bad to you. I like you a lot. you are
the best Teacher. I like you

We were going on our first field trip to see a stage play called *The Halloween Tree* by Ray Bradbury. Angela knew she would not be able to go unless she showed me she could follow simple classroom rules. I had given her the choice of having an adult from home accompany her because I was afraid I'd lose her among the hundreds of students at the theater. I found the following notes on my desk; the first one, dictated to a classmate, was written in script:

Dear Miss Kakugawa
Sorry I was late for class again. But all I want to do is go to the field trip please let my go. I won't be late anymore please let me go. Sorry. I love you.
Love,
Angela

The second note read:

To my teacher Miss Kakugawa,
can you give me another chance Let me go' to the Field trip For give me For coming in late starting today I KNOW
I will come in early I know you are made at me don't be mad at me Mrss Kakugawa I'm very sorry Jast give me one more chance That's all I want my Acnty and Uncle can't come To the play so let me "go."
Love,
Angela   Good-by ... love you

Angela did go to the play accompanied by our school counselor as her personal chaperone. Her aunt and uncle could not go and we knew how much Angela wanted to go with us.

Angela had come to us with no records from her previous school. She was, in fact, a complete stranger. One morning, the office clerk was sent to look after my class while I met with the principal, the counselor, a probation officer and her guardians, an aunt and uncle. Her aunt provided us with the following information:

Angela was born in prison to her aunt's sister, an unwed mother. Her maternal grandmother, who took her to Hayward, California, became the only mother Angela would know. The grandmother was illiterate and Angela grew up in the streets of Hayward. She was raped by an older brother, Joe, who was now in prison but soon would be released. Angela was placed in special education classes. One day, Angela kept a kindergarten child with her after school and as a result, the child's mother filed kidnapping charges against her. Angela was put in the Girls' Detention Home and sentenced to remain there until age 18 for as long as she lived in California. Her aunt and uncle had gone to Hayward to bring Angela back to Hawai'i. They found her in an isolated cell in the detention home. She was taken straight to the airport and was not allowed to say good-bye to her grandmother, whom she loved dearly.

A few days later she found herself in a strange home with an aunt, uncle and four cousins whom she had never seen before. The cousins were a result of two previous marriages of the aunt and uncle. The aunt expressed subtle hints of guilt over her niece's unfortunate life and the rape by her favorite nephew. There was also a touch of martyrdom as she came close to boasting of the expenses she had to bear as a result of bringing Angela into her home.

The counselor, principal and I chose not to look at each other because we were somewhat uncomfortable revealing the tears in our eyes. The image of Angela prevented from saying good-bye to her grandmother played liked a sad scene from a movie.

Angela was not in any way retarded; she had simply never benefited from caring and supportive teaching. I sought and obtained a verbal agreement from her aunt and uncle that Angela's academic progress would be secondary to her more crucial needs: to feel loved and become whole again.

Angela knew I had met with her aunt and uncle. She quietly asked me, "Do you know what happened to me?" I knew she was referring to her being raped so I simply answered, "Yes." I told Angela that I had discovered how much her aunt and uncle loved and cared for her. I wasn't sure of this, but felt Angela needed this. Angela asked, "Did they say they love me? Did you hear them say it? Was the principal there? Did she hear it, too?" I lied and said yes.

On her second day of school, Angela was going steady with a boy she had met in class on her first day of school and had written a threatening letter to a girl for liking the same boy.

Every morning I had the students write in their private journals. The purpose was twofold: to help them with their writing skills and help me gain more insights into their own world. I hoped to help Angela read and write through her journal. Her initial journal entries read as follows:

Dear Miss Kakugawa
"Hi"
I am Sorry Kakugawa I love you Do you like me yes or no I love you I am Sorry Good by I love you love you

Dear Miss Kakugawa
"Hi"
I love you a lot I cry and cry for you I am sorry Love is me
Good By
> *Love*
> *Angela*

Angela began to develop a great attachment to me. She'd come to me every morning to tell me how she felt. Although she couldn't write fluently, her journal became her second means of expression. Still, she continuously disrupted the class by playfully punching and teasing the boys.

She would dictate many letters to me, all directed to her grandmother whom she addressed as Mom. These letters were so pathetically painful to read and the message was always the same.

"Mom, I love you."
"Mom, I want you."
"Mom, I need you. Please come and get me. I want to go home."

I'd spend every spare minute I had explaining the situation to Angela. I didn't want to create a Santa Claus who didn't exist for her, so I tried to tell her that her Mom loved her, she was thinking of her right now but she could not return to Hayward just then. I tried every way I knew to help Angela see that a person's love for another doesn't stop with absence. I tried to help her visualize her mother thinking of her every morning when she got up. Through her comments and journal entries, Angela showed she didn't understand or couldn't understand this concept. I foresaw pain for Angela as I was beginning to see her strong growing attachment to me.

The Social Studies class was working on a research paper on a country. I told Angela she could do one by means of pictures. It was the first and only project she would complete with interest. She chose California. The other students knew California was not a country but they kept this information to themselves. She drew and labeled the state bird, tree and flower, using the encyclopedia like the rest of the class. She drew a map of California and wanted to know the exact location of Hayward. She was not satisfied with her picture collection and said, "I want words with mine, too." So she dictated and later copied a composition called "Why I Love California." "Because my mom is there" was the essence of her composition. I quietly watched another student give Angela a plastic covering for her work and observed her help Angela assemble her papers together with a title page. She received an E for Excellent for her work.

Angela's general lack of knowledge was very painful to witness. She didn't know who the President of the United States was at that time. She didn't know the difference between countries and states and didn't know how many states there were in the U.S. She only knew Hayward, California. I talked with her a lot, telling her facts I felt she needed to know. I wanted to protect her from the surprised looks she received from her peers at her lack of knowledge. I discussed current events with her as much as I could. Common knowledge — Christopher Columbus, George Washington, Abraham Lincoln, "Peanuts," current movie titles, actors and singers — all were foreign to her.

Being on recess duty became a stressful time for me because of the many physical fights she'd get into. She didn't know how to be a friend to others so she sassed and threatened instead. During one morning recess, I saw her punching, kicking and scratching a boy from another class. They were both crying and shouting obscenities at each other. I could see the streaks of bloody fingernail marks on both faces. With all of my 104 pounds, I tried to separate the two but failed. They were hysterically clawing and punching each other. My cries for help brought another teacher who was able to pull Angela off the boy. My colleague Linn lifted the screaming Angela off the ground while I sent the boy to the office. I tried to quiet Angela's crying and swearing by rubbing her back and softly repeating over and over, "Angela, you're all right. You're all right." She finally quieted down and I walked her to the office, all the while rubbing her back saying, "You're all right."

Linn would later tell me, "You gave me goose bumps at how you calmed that girl. I think you should adopt her. You're the only one who can save her. She needs you. I think your purpose in life is to save that girl." I felt anger toward Linn for the considerable responsibility she was trying to foist on me. I'd had my own thoughts about taking Angela in, but I didn't appreciate hearing them said aloud by someone else.

Every morning I'd look at Angela and I sensed her disposition. Most of the times her eyes would be clouded with sadness. On days like this, I'd motion her to come and she would draw up a chair very close to mine, our knees touching and we'd talk.

"Miss Kakugawa, please stop my dreams."

"What kind of dreams?" I asked.

"I still dream about Joe [her brother]. It happens over and over again in my dreams."

Sometimes she would say, "I love my brother but he did something bad." I could understand her confusion. I thought, Isn't one supposed to initially hate the person who did you wrong? Yet what happens if that person is someone you have loved all of your life? It seemed so simple to think of psychiatrists and therapists as a means to cure all of Angela's problems, but healing would not come easily.

The counselor was working closely with the probation

officer. Angela's uncle was with the military, so all medical help was provided by the military hospital. My two conferences with her aunt were fruitless endeavors because she spent the entire time saying how bad and incorrigible Angela was, the bad seed of the family.

Inside that streetwise exterior, Angela was a very sensitive and loving girl. For example, she'd notice my perfume and my hairstyle and often asked me, "Are you happy today? You look happy, Miss Kakugawa." One morning she drew a chair close to me and revealed:

"I tried to kill myself last night."

"How?" I asked her, trying to stay calm.

"I took a lot of pills. I took them from my aunty's medicine cabinet. I want to stop the dreams. Help me, Miss Kakugawa. Help me. Something's wrong with me."

I could only send her to the counselor with a note. I had 29 other students in my class. This became a pattern; she'd tell me what was going on and whenever I couldn't handle the situation immediately, I'd send the information and Angela to the counselor who was working very closely with her.

Angela was experiencing a lot of problems at home. For example, her cousins were using her as a scapegoat, accusing her of misdeeds and demanding she should be punished. In addition to her ongoing traumatic memories, her present world was one of survival among cousins who saw her as an intruder.

She'd dictate many letters to me, addressed to her uncle. Her message was always the same: "Uncle, I love you. I am afraid of you. I am bad. Hold me. I want you to hold me and love me." Sometimes these letters would be three pages long as she poured her heart out. She'd describe her cousins' treatment of her and her love-fear feelings toward her uncle. I don't know whether her uncle ever received these letters. On numerous occasions I mailed her letters to her grandmother in Hayward, but since she couldn't write, she would not send any letters back to Angela.

After a few months, Angela began to show me bruises and scratches on her arms and thighs, evidence of child abuse. I pointed out to Angela:

"Angela, we have laws that say no one can hit and hurt you like this. May I tell your counselor? If you say yes, the counselor will talk with your aunt and uncle. This is the only way I can help you."

She agreed, so I sent the following note to the counselor and received the accompanying note back:

Mary,
Can you check on Angela's story of being hit by aunt every day?
Thanks,
Fran

Fran,
Story has checked out re: this past weekend. Home life is pretty grim. Carey [our principal] *and I will be in touch with you.*
Mary

The bruises continued to appear. I also noticed bruises on her cousins. After a time, Angela refused to talk with me but her eyes told me how troubled she was. She'd enter the room with tears in her eyes. Finally she confessed, "I can't talk to you anymore. I got kicked out of the house last night. I don't know where I'm going tonight. Aunty said if I talk to you, she was going to sue you in court. I don't want to make trouble for you." I managed to convince Angela that this was not her problem but her aunt's and mine. She continued to confide in me.

Friday afternoons were especially difficult for Angela. She'd tell me, "I don't want to go home. I want to stay with you in school." She was not the only one I knew who hated Fridays and holidays. She cried the day before the Christmas holidays. I promised to write her two letters, one after Christmas and one after New Year's Day. I kept that promise. She thanked me privately for the letters when we returned to school in January. During the holidays, her aunt and uncle had somehow managed to legally adopt Angela. The counselor and I both knew another obstacle had been placed in our path. Angela refused to use her new name.

On January 6, I debated whether I should take a birthday cake to class for Angela's birthday, which was the following day. I was wary of taking in a cake for Angela because I knew I would not be able to do this for each of the students. I needed to be fair, I thought, so I decided against a cake. On the morning of her birthday, she walked in like a whipped animal. "Today's my birthday and no one at home wished me a Happy Birthday." I wished her Happy Birthday and gave her a hug. I told her that her day was not over yet. I wished then that I had had the courage to bring in that cake. I sent a note to the counselor about her birthday.

During the day, I sent Angela to the counselor so the class could make her birthday cards. I told them of her situation and her feelings of being a non-person. Every child in the class made a card. The boys, who tend to get silly over girls, impressed me with their messages of love and caring for Angela. Her bright smile upon receiving these simple tokens made us all feel good.

The next morning she told me her family had totally ignored her birthday. I had naively believed they were going to have a surprise birthday dinner for her and found it difficult to grasp the cruelty of such neglect. Her grandmother had called from Hayward but her uncle had purposely hung up just as Angela had gotten to the telephone. She told me she had always had a cake when she'd lived in Hayward.

Yet she asked, "Can I make a speech?" She stood awkwardly before the class and said with her head turned toward me for support, "Thank you for my birthday cards yesterday." She sat down, her face red with embarrassment.

I later discussed this with the class and told them how they had saved her birthday. I knew they felt good about themselves. I also knew the grapevine in school is very active and that my students knew more about Angela's background than they cared to reveal. This, I was sure, was the reason they showed such understanding, even though I was spending so much time and energy on Angela.

Angela's writing was improving through her journal. She was now attending special education classes in language, reading and math. I discussed her reading problems with her and asked if she wanted to learn to read. We began working with primers. She was beginning to read like a first grader. She'd occasionally say she was dumb so I was trying to change this self-image. Still, she continued to get into fights and continued to reveal herself in her journal.

I feel scare a lot Miss Kakugawa I Need you and I love you Miss Kakugawa I am scare
    1. but
    2. big
    3. be
    4. by
    5. bark
    6. best
    7. boy

My response was: *I will help you.*

Her second note read: *I feel Sad to day Do you Feel Sad to day you don't like me I cry and cry I need my mom — help me you don't like me.*

Her third note read: *I Feel Happy To Day Do you Feel happy Miss Kakugawa.*

During one of our class discussions, which we called "Heart to Heart Talks," the class pointed out with considerable insight how Angela never got into any fights with the students in our class. Our class was her home and family.

There were happy times when she'd tease and laugh and be happy. I would refer to her "Angela smile" which turned her entire face into one sunny bright day. She'd tease me about being single and having boyfriends. One morning she shared a dream she had the night before. She and I were at the beach together. We were both laughing and swimming and I was like a mother, she said. What a poignant dream, I thought, to replace that of Joe, her brother who had raped her. I had a thought that I would make that dream come true come summer.

Angela sought love in every way she knew. Love meant sexual love to her so she'd expend considerable energy in establishing a going-steady type of relationship with boys. The following note was sent to a boy in another class:

> *I know that you Don't love me But I love you. you are mad at me I am not mad at you good-By I Fucking love you But you Don't Fucking Don't love me I am soory I am soory I am soory I am soory Good-By Kiss me I love you*

Angela's best friend, Leesha, an African-American girl who was also a special education student, became her protector. Angela revealed her entire past to Leesha, which she kept secret. We three had to spend many recesses together because of Leesha's possessiveness that was engulfing their relationship.

The following notes were exchanged between the two girls:

*I am Sorry I love you you are my Best friend Do you love me
should good-by*
Angela

*I love you and I'm sorry But you have to under stand that no
Body is going to take me a way from you I'm going to stay with you
all times.*
Leesha

By March, I was feeling very good about Angela because she was beginning to talk about leaving me to go to the seventh grade. She'd speak of how she would come to see me sometimes after school, and I encouraged her to talk about going on to another school. Clearly, she was preparing herself for our eventual separation and I felt good about this. She continued to miss her "mom" and continued to write letters to friends in Hayward. The following letter, written in script, with an illustration of flowers weeping and bending to the ground, was addressed to her married sister, Kerri:

Dear Kerri,
*Hi I love you and I miss you do you love me yes or no tell my
mom I love her and tell Jason I love and miss him and tell Jimmy I
love and miss him.*
I love you all. I cry and I cry for you all. I need you,
*Kerri Kiss my neeces tell my neeces I love and miss them OK
Kerri I think I am going to die I am dumb Kerri I am crazy I want
to die now nobody love me and miss me you don't to my mom don't
love me my real mom don't love me I am sad to I am going to die
help Kerri*

Then one morning I found the following note on my desk, written after she'd been hit by her aunt.

I am sad do you Love me yes or no I am going to die good-By Love Angela

The teacher part of me could not help but notice how her need to express herself was teaching her to write. I sent the note to the counselor and made a decision myself. I asked to see the probation officer. I told him, "This child is being abused physically, emotionally and psychologically." I told him of her bruises, the punishment inflicted on her by her aunt and uncle on her birthday, and now this suicidal note. The probation officer's answer to me was that she wasn't being abused enough. She would need to show broken bones or damaged organs in order to have a case. He went on to say she would also have to run away at least six times. We would not be able to prove anything. I wanted to tell Angela, "Angela, run away six times and maybe I can help you."

At this time, Angela's aunt and uncle were having marital problems. One evening, Angela ran away from home with another child from school. When found, her aunt and uncle refused to take her back so she was placed in the Girls' Detention Home. How I wished I had had the foresight to give Angela my home telephone number but half of me was still afraid to become totally involved. I learned of her stay in the detention home the following day from the counselor. By this time, the counselor and I both knew our involvement with Angela was more than that of a counselor and a teacher.

The counselor took all day to obtain visitation rights for me to see Angela that afternoon and I was allowed an hour. I took two panties, a T-shirt, a pair of my shorts and my red hooded jacket. The harsh sterile concrete setting was depressing. They searched through my handbag and my package of clothing. Then they led me into a large cafeteria-sized room with a bare concrete floor and closed windows. Rough wooden benches and chairs were stacked against the walls. I heard a woman yell at the top of her voice, "Fontes! Move it here!" I watched Angela walk across the lawn toward the room. She looked whipped, sad and totally beaten. Her face lighted up with, "Miss Kakugawa!" She hugged and hugged me, then she moved her chair very close to mine before she sat down so her knees were touching mine. I let her talk and her words showed how she was trying to hold on to that world that promised her some love and some stability — school.

"You look pretty. Did you wear this to school today? What did you wear to school yesterday? Do the kids miss me?"

I answered each question. Then came the bombshell I was totally unprepared for: "I told them today that I don't want to go back to my aunt and uncle. He [the judge] asked me where would I go and I said that my teacher loves me. Miss Kakugawa, would you be my foster mother? I love you. I know you love me."

I fumbled with half-truths. I couldn't tell her that she would disrupt my personal life. Being single, I was afraid of the responsibility required and knew I would not be able to cope with Angela unless I had a therapist living with me, too. So I took the coward's way out and as the probation officer had done, I hid behind the law. I told her yes, I loved her, but I couldn't become her foster mother because we needed to operate within the law and the law right now made her a legal member of her aunt's and uncle's family. She half smiled and before I could finish, she said, as though she was expecting a no, "I know, I know." She quickly shifted attention to my package of clothes and was delighted. She had been wearing the same clothes for two days.

She pointed out her roommate, whom she said was a lesbian and had made overtures to her during the night.

I tried to make her understand about love. That one can love another even if they are apart. That even if she is not with her "mom," her "mom" still loves her. That out of sight doesn't mean out of mind. That I would always love her and would want to know about her life even when she was much, much older. I don't think she quite understood. I wanted to spare her any more feelings of rejection or being let down by those she loved. I knew she hated weekends because she believed I would forget her. I had the uncomfortable feeling that we would be parted soon, and I wanted to give her strength through some strong images for her to lean upon. How I wished she had an adult mind and didn't live only in the here and now.

After two days in the detention home and a day in court where she told the judge that she didn't want to return to her aunt and uncle, she was placed in a foster home. The counselor, a single parent with a daughter, had decided to take Angela in as her foster daughter. I offered to help her. We knew we were going to lose Angela fast after this if we didn't get personally involved. Her aunt and uncle refused our offer and instead threatened to sue the school for our interference. As a consequence, Angela was placed elsewhere. She would never learn how close she had come to having the counselor and me as her dual foster mothers.

I began to lose touch with Angela soon after this. She entered the foster home and returned to school after a few days, wearing my red hooded jacket. Her hair was neatly brushed and I felt inwardly pleased that someone out there was caring for Angela. I looked for signs to reassure myself that her world was better. Then she began to wear clothes inappropriate for a twelve year old. She looked almost seductive in her low-cut blouses and brief shorts. Her face told me we were losing her again. She looked like the child who had entered my room through the exit door that second day of school. Wild. She seemed to know this because she said, "I'm being bad, I know."

After a few days she said, "Something is not right. No one hits me anymore, but I don't feel right." I knew what she was saying — a stranger among strangers — how lonely and frightening it must be. This would be our last contact with each other.

The following day was the special education field day and Angela was out of my class for the entire day. I watched her from afar and saw her wearing an outfit far too mature for her. She had my red jacket tied around her waist even though it was a very hot day.

The next day I was on emergency leave to attend my grandmother's funeral on another island. I left on a Thursday afternoon and returned Monday morning. I returned to find Angela gone. She had been taken out of school on Friday and sent to another foster home on the other side of the island. My students shared with me how she had cried and had to be physically taken away. She left a hurriedly written note for me with the counselor that read, "Miss Kakugawa, I love you."

That was our good-bye and it hurt terribly to know that once again she was not allowed to say good-bye to someone she loved. God, I thought, won't there ever be closure in this child's life? During all these months, I had Angela working on a large wall collage mural for her bedroom. She was pasting happy faces cut out from magazines on an 18" x 24" poster sheet. The class finished the poster and we sent it to her new school. I wrote her a letter, assuring her of my love. Through the counselor, I heard of how she was a runaway again and again, going from one foster home to another.

In May, I asked for permission to see Angela on a week-end. The foster home denied my request. I was told she needed to adjust to her new home and her strong attachment to me would hinder the process.

When summer came, I had the freedom to bypass the bureaucratic lines of communication. I knew she was now in the Salvation Army Home for Girls and I called hoping to connect with her again. They refused to give me any names and my plea that I had been her teacher was to no avail. Angela was gone.

In June, during the last week of school, a student openly asked, "Miss Kakugawa, people who are single can't adopt children, can they?" I walked into that question weaponless. As the class looked at me in total silence, I explained single parenthood and how adoptions are now occurring in single households. Another voice asked, "Then why didn't you adopt Angela?"

I looked at this class who had never once complained about Angela, her disruptions or the special attention I had given her. Moreover, I had never discussed Angela's problems with them.

"How many of you feel I should have adopted Angela?" Every hand went up. Again I hid behind the law and explained our bureaucratic system. Then came this comment from a boy:

"Miss Kakugawa, you know that Angela loved you."

"Yes, I know."

Angela's last journal entry:

To Day I feel sad

Angela and her classmates left me a gift, a gift that came too late to be of help to Angela. They taught me to not only teach from my heart, but with a certain disregard to some of the rules society has imposed on us. They taught me that sometimes students' needs take priority over man-made rules.

After all, rules and laws are man-made so they can be changed. The following year I was put to the test.

Danny's mother was dying from cancer. I gave him a lot of special attention without the guilt I had felt with Angela. His mother was bedridden and Danny returned home each day, not knowing what he would find there. Every day I had my own private good-bye with him and I encouraged him to hug her every night and to express his love for her. Understandably, Danny was not doing his work, but I did not keep him in at recess to finish it as our class rules required. I felt he needed to be out every recess for some physical activities so, at least for 15 minutes, thoughts of his mother might fade somewhat from his mind. It wasn't long before students began to notice the privileges given to Danny, and two boys who had no love for homework approached me.

My answer to them was, "I have my own reasons for doing this. I will need Danny's permission before I can give you the whole story so can you please wait until I speak to him?"

Danny gave me the requested permission and I explained his situation to the two boys. The grapevine worked fast and soon I could sense growing kindness toward Danny from his classmates. When Danny lost his mother, I attended the funeral and in the back of the church, three of my most rascally and disruptive boys sat quietly in their white shirts, black pants and shoes. They had ridden on their bicycles to the service to be there for Danny.

It is so easy for teachers to underestimate their students' capacity for understanding and tolerance. If we allow them to do so, our students can help us teach with all of our instinctive senses and to bend the rules when it is necessary and prudent to do so. This brings humanity back to the classroom.

Over the years and with surprising frequency, students have taught me more than I have taught them. It is my belief that each student is capable of being totally trusted and honored with dignity. What is needed is to foster an environment for all these qualities to emerge from all of us. I say us because whatever it is we want out of our students, students also need these things from us.

Following is an open letter to Angela:

Dear Angela,

I'm sorry. I let you down, didn't I? I promised you I wouldn't let anyone hurt you anymore and you need never be afraid again. I promised I would always love you. I couldn't keep that first promise. I don't know where you are but maybe somewhere, someday, you will read this story and understand why I couldn't keep that promise to you. I'm still keeping that second promise.

Your teacher

On a September Morning

Speak not of
Broken promises,
Of drifting sand
And waves,
For time was all
That was granted us,
That endless
Summer's day.

From Sand Grains,
by Frances H. Kakugawa 🍎

4 | SPLIT-SECOND DECISIONS ON HIGH HEELS

Amy was a quiet sixth grader who was always absent on Jewish holidays. In class, she smiled her responses and seldom voiced her opinions. One day I heard a loud, "Fuck off!" The source was quiet, sweet Amy. A group of boys were around her desk and were teasing her to get her attention. Complete silence prevailed in our classroom as all heads turned to me. In particular, I saw the shocked look on Amy's face.

Wordlessly I motioned Amy to follow me out of the classroom. She was not only trembling but was near tears. I looked at her and quietly said, "Amy, that must have felt good." She burst into tears, held on to me and wept. After a few minutes, I asked her to go to the bathroom, and to return when she was ready. I came back to a very quiet classroom. When Amy walked in, her face was red from crying and I could almost hear the thoughts of the class, "Boy, the teacher must have really given it to her."

That was the beginning of a personal relationship between Amy and me. I, without much humility, later marveled at myself and could not believe the "natural" decision I had made. I learned to like myself a lot more that day. In fact, I taught with considerable joy in myself that day. That Christmas, our classroom won the $10 door-decorating prize. We had two doors decorated in celebration of Christmas and Hanukkah. Amy was clearly the source of our new knowledge of the Jewish faith and tradition.

Without these moments that demand on-the-spot

decision-making from us, teaching would become a dull, predictable, scripted world, with classrooms much like machines, divorced from the teaching-learning process.

Another student, Nicky, entered that same classroom. She had had a leg amputated because of cancer and she wasn't able to let any of us forget that. Her attitude, "but I have cancer, you know, so I need special treatment," confused her classmates. They knew Nicky deserved some empathy, but they didn't appreciate her attitude and I could sense a socially unacceptable situation developing for Nicky. Whenever new students arrived, they tried to be helpful by carrying her books between classrooms, but they soon got tired of that.

Our class was invited to recite our poems at the State Curriculum Fair at the Blaisdell Center. I could take only 20 students so I announced I would select 20 of our best poems and the authors of the poems would attend.

Nicky wanted to be one of these poets, but her poem was not selected. She was the only student who came to me with, "Why didn't you choose my poem?" Rather than trying to come up with an answer, I looked at her and suggested, "Why don't you write me more poems?" Her new poems were about flowers, butterflies and rainbows so I continued with, "Write more, Nicky." She looked at me and said, "Why aren't you choosing my poems?" I took a deep breath and told her gently, "Nicky, these are not good enough." I asked her, "Nicky, why don't you write about things that are very close to your heart? Something that you think about a lot when you're alone and have deep feelings for." She looked directly at me and asked almost defiantly, "You mean like my cancer?" I replied, "If that's what you feel deeply about, yes." She asked to stay in for morning recess complaining, "I don't know how to start." I suggested, "Maybe you could begin with how it was before you got cancer." She wrote continuously for 15 minutes and when the recess bell rang, she had written the following poem, one that needed no editing:

Life

Before I could run
Through the big white fields.
Before I could skip like a stone over water.
Before I could hang on the bars
Like all the other girls.
Before I could play dodge ball
And climb a banyan tree.

Then my doctor came in
With a strict look on his face.
He said, "This is a horrible disgrace.
Next week on Tuesday, your leg will be gone.
The test shows cancer has come along."
My leg is now gone,
I feel lonely and sad.
Does God still love me?
Pain is what I have.
I'm going to succeed
Because I have hope.
I've discovered I can write
Of my feelings and my fears.
I'm glad I can let others know how I feel.
I'm glad I can read my poems,
It helps a great deal.
It's time for me to sing
Another song.

We went to the cafeteria to practice our readings. Nicky struggled up to the front with her crutches as her classmates had learned not to offer assistance. Each time she began, she would burst into tears and be unable to recite her poem. Finally I took a deep breath and said from the back of the cafeteria, "Nicky, are you standing there as a girl with cancer or as a poet? I'm taking only poets to the Blaisdell Center." The entire cafeteria came to a silent standstill. She looked angrily at me and said, "Poet." I said, "Good. Let's hear from the poet." She recited her poem without hesitation to its end.

Two girls came to me after our practice and said, "Miss Kakugawa, that was good what you did with Nicky. She really needed that." I thanked the girls and shared with them my own unsure feelings and the risk I had taken that day at the expense of being perceived as mean. They assured me that I had done the right thing.

At the Blaisdell Center, Nicky created a dramatic scene by haltingly working her way up to the microphone on her crutches and after she recited her poem, there was not a dry eye in the auditorium.

Before the poetry reading was over, I had to take a dose of my own medicine. The class had insisted I also memorize my poem for the occasion and the rascals had insisted on my lengthy two-and-a-half page poem entitled "A Tin Man's Tears," which appears in the chapter "Hickory Dickory Dock." During our practice sessions, I never completed a recitation without fumbling and having complete mental blackouts. By then, each student had memorized my poem and would mouth the words when I drew a blank. When I stood in front of the microphone that day, I was momentarily so moved by what I saw, I had to choke back my own tears. All the students facing me in the front row sat there with their fingers crossed. I did not let them down. I am a poet.

Being human, not all my classroom decisions were something to write home about. There were many times when my high heels wobbled and cracked as I made on-the-spot decisions on my feet. For example, Emi was a beautiful first grader in my class when I was teaching in Jackson, Michigan. She had a face that artists could have used for paintings of angels. But, a good part of the time, her beauty was covered with dirt. Her neck showed evidence of weeks of accumulation of dirt and not having had a bath. Her blond hair was matted with oil and dirt. I could sense her presence the moment she entered the room because of the odor of urine.

One day, during our reading circle, she was making a lot of errors and I totally lost my own dignity. I said to her, "Emi, you read like you look. Look at you. Your hair is uncombed. There's dirt on your face. You read sloppily, you skip a lot of words. You are a mess!"

I did not know my principal, Miss Clarke, had entered my classroom at the very moment I had uttered those reprimands. She looked at me kindly and said, "I'll take care of this," and walked out with Emi.

Before long, Miss Clarke's voice came over the intercom, "Miss Kakugawa, Emi is ready to return to your classroom." Emi entered the room with her hair combed and flowing loosely around her shoulders. Her face was scrubbed and she had a most gigantic ribbon on her head. The class all gasped. I looked at Emi and said, "You look like a princess." The class chorused, "You look so pretty."

Emi's face was all aglow. I continued to call her Princess for the rest of the year. Miss Clarke later told me the only ribbon she had was from an azalea plant on the office counter.

Before the year was over, I learned that Emi lived in a trailer with no hot water and bathing facilities. About twice a month, she would go to her Grandma's to take a bath. Emi's father was an alcoholic. During one of our mother-teacher conferences, I had arrogantly suggested to Emi's mother, "Why don't you leave this man? Look at what he's doing to you and your children?" And she answered, "But I love him." She taught me to not impose my values onto others.

I also learned why only one parent attended our programs intended for both. Emi told me their car could seat only one passenger and the car had no floor. She felt it was a special car because they could throw their litter to the floor, where it would fall right through to the ground.

Emi taught me that for every behavior, there is a reason, sometimes beyond the control of the child. How dare I impose one set of expectations on all children without knowing the whys. How dare I not be each child's companion and guide instead of judge? How dare I base my decisions on my own ignorance?

Nine years after my year in Jackson, I returned for a visit. One teacher friend had gathered all my former first graders, now high school sophomores, in her living room as a surprise. Emi was there, beautiful as ever with a radiant smile. I felt I had been forgiven. And on that hot summer's day, they all sang "Mele Kalikimaka," the Hawaiian Christmas song, which they had learned during their first-grade year with me.

Citing one's humanity can easily become a poor excuse for our failings if we continuously fail. Emi left a shadow in my memories for years. I had forgotten the promise I had made myself during my third year of teaching. My niece, Jill, was a first grader in my class. I had named her when she was born and she was very special to me. During that year, I did not raise my voice once, thinking I couldn't do so with Jill in the room. I was kind and loving all year. Because I needed additional help, I told myself to imagine a TV camera in my room at all times and that my behavior was being linked to a public screen.

Was this a cure-all? No. It became natural and easier when I stopped using gimmicks and people outside of myself and relied on my own resources. Each time I raised my voice or lost my temper in front of my students, I scraped away a bit of my own dignity in the eyes of my students. Each time I made a decision that degraded a student, I also degraded myself. Whatever I did, I did to myself.

A kindergarten student tried to tell me this during my first year of teaching, but I didn't hear him. Arnold, with a defeated look in his eyes said, "When I'm at home, I get yelled at. When I'm in school, you yell at me." I put my arm around his shoulders and defensively but gently said, "But I don't yell at you. I only use a loud voice." Who was I kidding?

The teacher does not have sole rights to the decision-making process in the classroom. My sixth-grade language arts class was comprised of all boys, most of them taller than me, and they were boys who loved sports and girls much more than they did literature. I began my class by going to the board with my back to the class when one student interrupted me with, "Miss Kakugawa …" And I, without turning, said, "Wait, let me finish this first." I continued to be interrupted with, "Miss Kakugawa," and I continued to say, "Wait." Finally one student came up to me quietly and whispered, "Miss Kakugawa, there's blood on your skirt."

Embarrassed, I turned to look at my skirt, glanced quickly at all the boys and said, "I'll be right back." I ran to the office red-faced where the staff washed my skirt and dried the wet spot with a hair dryer while I readied the rest of me for class. I returned to a very quiet and orderly room and not a word was said as I continued my lesson. I was too embarrassed to say anything.

I expected the grapevine to go haywire after class because these were the kinds of boys who teased others mercilessly and now they were armed with something that could cause great embarrassment to their teacher. No references were ever made to my soiled skirt. I looked at the boys the following day and said, "Thank you for yesterday." No comments were heard except for a silence that seemed to say, "We understand." Or perhaps their silence meant, "We are too embarrassed for you to say anything." Being a younger teacher then presented its own kinds of problems.

It becomes obvious that the teacher is not the only one making constant decisions in the classroom. As they have shown us, students, too, meet up with unforeseen situations where they also need to make split-second decisions. It must be simpler for a teacher to make decisions since she or he is a body of one. As in the above anecdote, how did an entire class make a split-second decision to tell me quietly of my soiled dress and how did they, as a group, decide to keep the incident private?

How often have students decided not to express themselves in class because of peer pressures? How often have students decided not to give the true reasons for their lack of participation to preserve their dignity? How often have students elected to keep the truth from us with their silence because they felt it would not be fairly received by us? How often have students spared us with their decisions?

So it seems that we are constantly in mental movement — both students and teachers. Just as I have often made decisions for my own comfort rather than for the benefit of my students, because of my fear of entering unexplored territory, so do students experience similar situations. Often the most crucial decisions are not centered on complex educational theories but simply on whether one should or shouldn't take a birthday cake to class. And often, these are the hardest decisions to make. ●

5 | TEACHER, YOU LOOK LIKE A HORSE!

No College of Education course will ever prepare anyone for the genuine, unpredictable, uncensored responses teachers get in kindergarten and first-grade classrooms. Professors who make it a requirement for future teachers to write unit lesson plans on every subject would be well advised to work in a kindergarten class, so they won't demand lesson plans that have to show predicted student and teacher's responses. Not all youngsters will follow the script of unit plans. After first grade, they learn to grit their teeth and let teachers teach, oftentimes mechanically, their lesson plans without having the opportunity to say, "Those are your plans but that's not where we're at."

Once a kindergarten child brought an African snail to class, so I quickly took out a photo of an African snail from my picture file. I also knew a snail song we could dramatize in a dance. Teacher-perfect, according to my plans. During our discussion, I pointed to the antennae of the snail and one little boy asked, "Teacha, get TV inside, huh?" No, no, child. Your response should have been silence so I could have gone on displaying my expertise on the snail and progressed on to the dance.

What child goes through school without a farm unit? One year, we were all sitting in a circle in front of our farm bulletin board when a first grader pointed to a specific part of the cow's anatomy and asked, "What's that?"

"That's the udder and those are teats," I smugly responded. Ah, a great way to begin the discussion on the cow!

Thank you, child! Then I heard her murmur, "Oh, the poor cow. She has to chew down there," followed by a chorus of "Yeah, the poor cow." (In Hawai'i Creole English, or pidgin, the plural of "teeth" often sounds like "teats.")

Professor, where are you now? These moments can be fun, except for those times when the principal sits in the back of the room with his evaluation form and one silently prays to no avail, "Please kids, keep to my script so I can get a good evaluation."

I got up a half-hour early one morning so I could French-braid my hair. It was the "in" hairdo of the time. Feeling very chic and rather Parisian, I walked into my kindergarten class at Laupāhoehoe School on the Big Island. One child ran into the classroom, stopped short in front of me and exclaimed, "Teacher, you look like a horse!" I should have slept that extra half-hour. That was the first and last French braid I have ever worn.

One morning during our "share and tell" period in first grade, the principal walked in just as a child was talking about her father's cataract surgery: "He has catholic in his eyes." I was too inexperienced to have burst out laughing.

Children after first grade become more sophisticated and will voice expressions they view to be uncomplimentary, sotto voce. So teachers have to have their antennae up at all times. One day I walked into my third-grade class feeling beautiful with newly permed hair that had cost me more than $90. One student quickly noticed and said, " You curled your hair. You look nice." I thanked him and added like a kid wanting more attention, "I'm glad someone noticed."

Ryan, who was writing in his journal at his desk mumbled, "I can never tell if she has a new hairdo because her head always looks like a triangle." (Ryan, you get an A for transferring your geometry knowledge into your daily living without my blessing.)

During recess, Miss Sato was rushing down the stairs for yard duty when a kindergarten girl, who was rushing up the stairs, stopped her and announced excitedly, "Miss Sato, Miss Sato, you're growing a moustache!" Unfortunately, or fortunately, a teacher from our car pool overheard the child. That story was shared in our after school car pool. The next morning, all four of us were sleepily quiet on the drive in to school until Karen asked, "Well? Did all of you rush out to get some Nair?" I knew then I had not been the only one checking for facial hair that morning.

Children's perceptions and their honest responses arising from innocence are the stories most taken home by teachers, to share around the dinner table or in the teachers' lounge the following day. They sometimes bring tears because children do not live with innocence alone, but often with the wisdom of Solomon.

Falling in love is everything that poets and songwriters claim it to be. Unfortunately, so is falling out of love. I was a supervisory teacher at an elementary school; I had no classes to call my own but visited schools in the district. My office, so to speak, was a desk in a multipurpose room which students passed by daily to go from one classroom to the other. One day, a kindergarten girl passed me, retraced her steps, stood and looked at me. Then she asked, "Are you feeling sad?"

I said, "Yes." She cradled her arms as if holding an infant and said, "Don't be sad. When you were a baby, your mommy loved you." Then she went on to her class.

I inquired about this little girl and learned that she was living with her father and stepmother and was having problems adjusting to the changes in her life. A year later I saw her on crutches, her body twisted by spinal tuberculosis. I have never forgotten her for she was the only one who had stopped to help me in my moment of private despair.

Five children helped me establish the basis for my entire teaching career. In my second year of teaching, I was having parent-teacher conferences with parents of my first graders. Five parents told me, "My son (daughter) comes home and says, 'I'm the teacher's pet.'" It was then that I made a decision. I will teach so every child in my class will believe he or she is my favorite student. There will be none of that lukewarm fairness in the classroom, but rather that passion that will make each child feel, "I am her favorite." And no child can feel this unless a private relationship develops and is sustained between the student and the teacher, even if she looks like a horse. 🍎

6 | HICKORY DICKORY DOCK

Dead Poets Alive

It was the dead who kept me alive
During all those years growing up
Confined in a village so isolated,
The only communication lines:
An unpaved road sans cars,
A battery-run radio,
Three community telephones.

It was the dead who took me beyond
The catalogs of Sears and Montgomery Ward,
Dream-makers of that remote village,
When one day I discovered an oracle
Within the pages of poets long gone,
Promising a wondrous world
For the me not yet formed.

Memorizing lines from "Thanatopsis,"
Reciting Poe's "Annabel Lee,"
Aching with Elizabeth Barrett Browning's
"How Do I Love Thee?"
Dreaming in isolation
With Emily Dickinson.
Yes, Yes, I said.

Believing in Sara Teasdale's
Life has loveliness to sell,
Impatient to meet those two roads diverged
Knowing I could not travel both.
Fantasizing sinking a thousand ships,
And becoming a phantom in delight,
Made me wish for two mornings a day.

Yes, yes,
It was the dead who gave me dreams
Forming the woman I would become
Long before I became.
But oh, how I wandered
Lonely as a cloud.

Frances H. Kakugawa

Poet Georgia Heard asked in a workshop, "When did you start becoming a poet?" When? For me it began at Pohoiki on the Big Island of Hawai'i. I spent all my childhood summers there, camping with family and friends. There was a tree that I sat in, watching the waves as they tumbled in to shore. I sometimes held a book in my hand, but most of the time, I leaned my body into the sturdy branches, balancing so I would not fall, watching the waves. It was then that I began being a poet.

I began again in Jackson, Michigan, where I lived with my pen pal. I had a room up in the attic and one afternoon, I looked out and saw the fall leaves slowly falling past my window and I began to hear in my head, the soft piano music of Roger Williams playing "Autumn Leaves." For the first time, I knew the essence of that song in my new environment.

When winter came, I remember walking alone in the freshly fallen snow. I kept looking behind me to see the footprints I left in the snow. I felt so sad, thinking, "This is so beautiful, yet I can't do anything to preserve this." I drove to school passing the frost-covered branches and I ached with its beauty. Then, too, I began being a poet.

Then one summer I fell in love. I gave him the poem "How Do I Love Thee" by Elizabeth Barrett Browning. In return he gave me the poem "The Road Not Taken" by Robert Frost. Then he left. I read and read "Reflections on a Gift of Watermelon Pickles." I played Kui Lee's record "I'll Remember You." I began to write poems to keep from dying. All this was my genesis as a poet and I have not stopped being one, nor shall I ever.

This could have been written in poetic form. The message is, poets are not always poets because of the poems they write but because of what is inside of them and because of the connections between their inner selves and the world around them. Poems are gifts that come to us to be written.

Some years ago, I got a letter from a former first grader from Michigan who was a wife and mother of four. After she had just seen her children off to school on the bus, she wrote, "For the first time, I realized what you were trying to tell us in first grade. Only this morning did I see all this beauty around me. I looked out my kitchen window and suddenly, it seemed as if I had a new pair of eyes. And I thought, "This is what my first-grade teacher was talking about." At that moment she began being a poet.

Wendy Weaver discovered this about herself in third grade and I was privileged to be there. We were working on haiku poems, focusing on images and recognizing the powerful use of language by the great haiku poets of Japan such as Basho and Issa. Imagine creating all those images with only 17 syllables. Imagine also that all the language needed to help us create these images is available at our fingertips. "Look at these books," I announced. "These books have all won the Nobel Prize and the Pulitzer Prize. These are the highest awards a writer can receive. Yet every word in these books is in this classroom right here. They're all in this dictionary. All that these writers did was to bring these words together to create that image they wanted or to create that character, that scene or that plot that they wanted in their books. And you have these right here with you."

In the midst of this, Wendy excitedly said, "I know what to write. I know what to write. A few years ago, my family and I were traveling by train and I saw this beautiful winter scene outside my window and I had felt so sad because I couldn't do anything about it. Now I can." Wendy's haiku:

> *White snow on the ground,*
> *It is the quiet morning.*
> *The train is passing.*

Wendy took that morning to discover the poet that existed inside of her and she has never stopped being in touch with all the pain and ache and beauty that go with being a poet. She discovered what it is to be a poet when she found a poet is not one who puts words down on paper but one who is able to see one's life in relation to the world within and outside of herself; to be able to make sense of her world. When she spent a year in France as a student from Wheaton College, her e-mail letters were full of poetic images and soul-filled descriptions and perceptions as she traveled throughout the country.

Students become poets by getting in touch with their poetic heartbeat and awareness — before taking that pen or pencil in their hands. Otherwise, writing poems can easily become a mechanical exercise. Nineteenth-century writer Okuma Kotomichi said it best:

"Poems are not written to sing of the moon and flowers; they must speak of our hearts in response to the moon and flowers. We must never forget that in our hearts are the seeds of our poems. If we merely speak of moon and flowers, poems become simply poetical forms, whatever the human heart may be. If these things become a part of ourselves, then we may admire them in verse."

Students also need a wealthy source and use of language to help bring their poetic images, feelings and thoughts to paper, like Wendy who had to discover the form of a haiku to be able to complete her poetic experience. Students need to experience language at every stage of their lives. Wendy's father didn't stop reading to Wendy until she was in high school so her first encounter with classical literature came through her father's voice. The conversations in our real world are so limited because we seldom change our sentence structure or vocabulary in everyday conversations, speaking instead in highly formulated ways. It is through literature that we experience the powerful and expressive possibilities of language in various forms.

When I had my first book of poetry published, I was surprised to discover it was being used in English classes in high schools and in colleges. I had not taken any courses in writing or poetry. "What do you see in my poems?" I asked one high school teacher and she began listing all the poetic images and literary devices present in my poems. I had to use the dictionary to discover what an allegorical poem was, as I had no idea I had used this technique in what I had written.

When I had composed those poems, I wrote to express my feelings and thoughts without giving any attention to the devices employed. By definition, I didn't know what these poetic devices were; I only knew them through the actual use of language from the years of reading I had done during my childhood and throughout my adult life.

I would later understand why certain students who had only a dictionary knowledge of literary devices, grammatical rules and punctuation marks, were not able to use them in their writing. To be able to do this, they needed to experience, explore and become totally immersed in the actual use of language in their writing.

What is a poem? This was best defined by a class of kindergartners at Mt. View School on the Big Island. I was invited as a practicing poet to help them write poems. After being introduced as such, I asked, "Do you know what a poet does?"

"Write poems!" came the answer in unison. "Do you know what a poem is?" I asked. This was met with complete silence and so I waited. Finally one little voice piped up:

Hickory, Dickory, Dock.
The mouse ran up the clock.
The mouse ran down,
The clock struck one.
Hickory, Dickory, Dock.

Another voice added:

Mary had a little lamb
Its fleece was white as snow.
And everywhere that Mary went,
The lamb was sure to go.

I got chickenskin all over from these replies. "Yes," I said, "You know what a poem is." These five-year-olds had demonstrated they knew the difference between a poem and a narrative. No one mentioned *The Three Billy Goats Gruff* or *The Three Little Pigs*, but rather they began reciting nursery rhymes.

I wanted to congratulate the people in these children's lives who had read to them. This was in early fall and these students had not yet learned to read so it wasn't through form that they knew the difference between a poem and narrative. They knew which was which through the use and knowledge of language. Linguist Michael Halliday said it best when he wrote that the child knows what language is because he knows what language does.

At the end of my visit, the children had all written poems capturing various images. And they all shouted, "Yes!" when I asked them, "You didn't believe me when I said there's a poet in each one of you and today, we were bringing that poet out. Well, did you bring that poet out?"

How did I help to bring that poet out? I began by having the children close their eyes and I read a haiku. I then asked them to describe what they saw in their minds. These are images, I explained, or pictures that we see inside our head. And this is what writers do; they use words to describe these pictures or images in our head. Sometimes, it's best to think of our readers as blind people. They can't see, so we need to use words to conjure our visions in their heads.

They sat with their eyes closed and began to shout out the images they saw. "I see an image of a cloud." "I see an image of a giant monster." One little boy in a frightened, trembling voice said, "Teacher, I see only black." I asked him gently, "What is your favorite food?" He said, "Spaghetti."

"Can you see that spaghetti?" "Yes." "Good, now close your eyes and see the image of your favorite spaghetti." His shoulders relaxed and he began sharing other images with his eyes closed. And thus began his first step toward poetry writing.

One first grader on the island of Kaua'i taught me that sometimes one needs to begin with the very concrete. When I walked into a first-grade classroom by invitation, I saw a group of teachers sitting in the back of the room with body language that said, "Okay, show us what you can do." Within minutes I realized that English was the second language for the students gathered for my poetry session. We began with the three-line haiku poem and moved on to images.

We all went outdoors to look for an image that we could bring into the classroom for our first poem. One little boy returned happily into the classroom with his fist clenched. " Teacha, teacha, I have my image," and he slowly opened his fist to show me a dead brown leaf. "Tell me about this leaf," I prodded him. "Fall down from tree." "Where did it fall?" "To the ground, teacha." "How did it fall? Fast? Slowly?" "Slow… slow," he answered. "What color is your leaf?" "Brown." "Can I write down what you just told me?" "Yeah."

To keep with the three-line haiku form I wrote:

A brown leaf falls
Slowly, slowly
To the ground.

His first poem was very similar to the three-line haiku poems I had used as models.

In writing, we experiment with various uses of language. To the line, "A leaf falls," students describe what they see and they describe a variety of images. Then to the line, "A red maple leaf slowly falls into a stream and floats away," their images are more precise and closer to the image of the writer. If we want our readers to see the details of our writing, we will need to use language to create these images in their heads.

We then use language to show how a supposedly poor writer would use language as compared to a successful writer. To further explore the value of more precise images, we often took the role of the just-average writer and purposely used words like "beautiful, good and nice" to show how such bland, generic adjectives fail in creating vivid images. Students then begin to sense the powerful and functional uses of language.

It is always a golden moment when students learn, "I am a poet." On one occasion, I visited a fifth-grade class that was involved in writing poems. One student lay his head down and kept this position while others all around him began writing. He didn't look very happy so I approached him with, "How are you feeling?" Silence. I pursued with, "I have a feeling you're not happy with this. Are you wishing maybe you were somewhere else?"

He looked at me suspiciously and nodded. "Good," I said. "Poets do best when they write about their real feelings and thoughts. Where would you rather be?" He mentioned a few places. I continued with "Why don't you write about that — how you'd rather be somewhere else than being here with me?"

He wrote a poem beginning with "I wish I were somewhere else." I asked if he would share it with the class. He asked, "Is it good?" I said, "Very good. You're a good writer." He asked me to read it so I did and the class applauded. That was the start of the river's flow. He wrote for the rest of the period. When the bell rang, he came to me and said, "Thanks" and walked out.

His teacher asked me, "What did you do to him? This is the first time he has ever shown interest in his work." I answered, "I did not deny him his feelings." She then gave me some background; he was living with an alcoholic single parent. I had to deny myself feelings of wanting to follow him to see that he would have a good life.

Discovering one is a poet can often mean having one's own therapist. One day I found a piece of paper folded into four on my desk. On it was the following poem:

Change

My family isn't the same anymore.
My mother doesn't get enough love
She says. She only told me.
She loves someone new
And I don't know what to do.
Soon, in March, I'll have a new place,
New friends to meet, a new father
To spend the rest of my life with.
Oh God, help me please.
Please just put my mind
At ease.

I counseled Tracy as she cried and shared her uncertainties and fears because her mother had told her the day before that she was having an affair. She asked me to keep her poem between us. The next day, Tracy and I had another session together to explore her feelings. At the end of the session I asked Tracy, "Did you know you wrote a pretty good poem?" She asked, "I did?" and seemed so pleased. Ah, I thought, the person versus the creator.

The next day Tracy approached me with, "Was that really a good poem I had written?" I said, "Yes." She said, "You can put my poem on the bulletin board and you can also print it in our poetry book." We discussed the personal nature of her poem and we both decided that perhaps we needed to clear this with her mother.

Her mother's reaction was, "Dear God, I can't let my husband find out." Her mother and I had a session on the creative process and how the source of writing is not always real-life experiences, but can also come from a writer's imagination, ideas or other vicarious experiences. I showed her one of my poems about childbirth and explained, "I am single. I wrote this poem about giving birth. Did I have a baby or was my source less personal?"

The following day she sent me a note thanking me for explaining the creative process and for letting her read my own published books of poetry. Her decision was, "By all means, Tracy should have her name on her poem."

We published our anthology of poems and at our poetry reading and autograph party, Tracy's mother and father were in the audience. They thanked me for showing Tracy a whole new world of writing. They saw her as a poet.

I, too, had to discover for myself what my students and their parents had to learn. When I had my first book of poems published, I cried to a friend, "But they don't understand," referring to some public responses. Her wise answer was, "Could it be that they can't understand? This is the risk you took when you went public. Once you publish a poem or have a reader, the poem is no longer yours."

In my book *Sand Grains*, the following poem appears:

Boy Into Man

I hold his hand
And softly cry

Not yet, not yet.

But even little boys
Need to be free.

I feel him slip
Away from me —

Tiny, scrubby, enormously brave.

And without a glance
To where I stand,

He enters the room
Alone.

A colleague informed me that she couldn't leave my book lying around in her living room because of her young son. She didn't realize her son was capable of having such nasty sexual thoughts, she said, and she'd discovered this with a comment he had made about my book. She was referring to the poem "Boy Into Man." She explained, "My son said, 'She's talking about going into the bathroom,'" referring to the last line in the poem.

This poem was also used as a theme for an open house in a school district in California.

When I had my first autograph party for *Sand Grains*, a parent of one of my first-grade students looked through the book, quietly put it down and said before walking away, "I didn't know you wrote this kind of poems." He was a Christian minister. How did I handle this? With the quiet vengeance of the young.

His daughter Beth wrote a poem beginning with "Miss Kakugawa, Taking a shower," and she had illustrated it accordingly, a nude Miss Kakugawa under a showerhead. Her mother came in, apologizing for the shameful poem her daughter had written. She explained how Beth had used nudity and she had already disciplined her daughter. I replied that she had done a wonderful job of finding a rhyming word for Kakugawa. To my "What's wrong with this?" Beth's mother explained that she herself is never seen in the nude and that she always closes her door when she dresses. I put Beth's poem on the bulletin board.

What can a teacher do but turn to the great classical artwork of our times? I had a unit on art, covering Van Gogh, Michelangelo and other artists. In December I had a painting of Baby Jesus, nude, held by Mary. No one blinked an eyelash; the children didn't, nor did the student's parents.

Wendy, Tracy and other students discovered the power of poetry and found solace, pleasure and great satisfaction in their exploration. They learned that the creative source of writing freed their work from being judged as personal confessions. This knowledge comes from how other writers and their works are explored, for they know if we do not separate the person from the poet then they, too, will be so judged.

How do we get the best out of writers? Perhaps it is best for all teachers who work with students' writing to personally experience the process of writing themselves. When I was teaching, the state writing assessment program recommended that third graders describe their bedrooms as an exercise in descriptive writing. Not all children have their own rooms while others may be living in vans or elsewhere. To protect their own dignity, many students will not tell you that they have no source for such descriptive writing.

One year I decided to do descriptive writing of my own room and found it impossible to do. It was too broad an assignment. My favorite advice has been, "Write about one tree or one blade of grass and leave the forest alone." Assign me to describe a tiny part of my room and I'll be able to write about that special pillow on my bed, made by a dear and now departed friend. How can we expect our students to write about topics that we as teachers find difficult to do — we who've been alive so much longer?

It becomes very crucial that teachers and writers understand the source of writing. I did volunteer work at a public library when a request came in from high school students who needed help in their writing. These were students who had a passion for writing but felt unfulfilled as writers in their classrooms.

Lisa, a ninth grader, came in chewing and cracking her gum. She threw her handbag on the table in front of me and a pack of cigarettes fell out. She then showed me her poems, each one of which dealt with love and sex. I ignored everything I saw except her poems. I commended her on some of the strong images in her poems. When I had seen her cigarettes and heard her cracking gum, I knew I was being tested. We went straight to the poet in her, nowhere else.

I recommended other poets she would enjoy since she seems so interested in love. She was surprised she was not the only one writing about love. The following week, she was in the poetry section of the library, looking for poetry books.

One afternoon, she threw a poem down at me saying, "I wrote this while waiting for you." It was a poem with very vivid images describing a child with tears on her face, swinging on a swing. She explained, "I was walking to the library when I saw a girl on a swing and it bothered me to see this girl crying because I usually think of children being happy on a swing."

She then took out a purple ceramic cow and said, "I need to write a poem about this for tomorrow's assignment." I looked at her cow, at the poem she had written and suggested that she take that poem in instead. "No," she said, "I can't do that. My assignment is to write a poem about this cow, so help me." She wrote a dead poem and I suggested that she take both poems in and explain to the teacher about her experience of seeing that child on the swing. "No," She said, "I can't do that."

What she was saying was she was not allowed to tap her own resources to write a poem but was forced to use the teacher's imposed subject. Writers write best when their own sources of experiences, ideas, feelings and thoughts are tapped. The ceramic cow was imposed upon her and Lisa was forced to write from outside of herself.

Tiffany came in, verbalizing all the characters and plot in a novel she was planning to write. She spoke of poems she was going to write. For more than a month, she verbalized her intentions but did not bring in anything in print. I told her I would not be meeting with her anymore since she had not been writing. She shook with nervousness and said, "But I can't let you read my stuff because it matters to me what you think of me."

Ah, I thought. *The fear of being judged.* We discussed the source of writing as being real or imagined. She stood up and was jubilant. She then paused and said, "I can't be a good writer because I'm not allowed to swear. "She disclosed her limitations, that she was a Christian and was not allowed to use strong language. The best-sellers today were full of expletives, she pointed out. How could she write like that with her religious background?

"Tiffany," I said, "give me an example." She explained, "A character gets upset and swears the F-word to make an impression. I can't use the F-word." "Tiffany," I said, "Why did that writer have that character use the F-word?" Tiffany's response was, "He wanted to show how angry that character was." I continued, "Tiffany, is that the only way you can show anger in a character?"

Tiffany stood up and walked back and forth and punched one hand into the other and described her behavior as a very angry person. She jumped a few times, excited at the revelation, and exclaimed, "I know what you're saying! I know what you're saying! I can use body language or other language! Thank you. Thank you!"

That was the beginning of her writing. All it took was to look at the writing process as:

1. A writer taps his or her own resource of ideas, feelings, thoughts and experiences, real or imagined.

2. A writer's only tool is language.

3. With language, the writer transforms his or her resources into a symbolic form such as a poem, story, play, nonfiction, etc.

4. A reader brings meaning to this symbolic form with his or her own resources of ideas, feelings, thoughts and experiences, real or imagined, often referred to as prior knowledge.

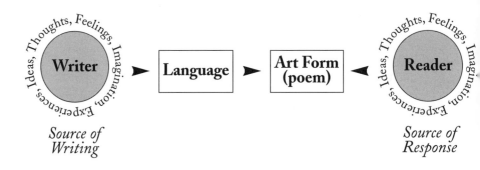

Source of
Writing

Source of
Response

And the writing begins.

There can be a Catch-22 in working with writers. Students are encouraged to write honestly and freely from their poetic souls and when they do, we receive them with our own and it can be a painful, joyful, beautiful experience. I felt all my students' pain and beauty late one night while reading their poetry and could not go to sleep until I wrote the following to release my own thoughts:

A Tin Man's Tears

The light from my fluorescent lamp
Magnifies the order of disarray across my desk.
I sit and stare, page after page of poetic lines,
Assignments written in class today.
A child's "I'm all poemed out"
Keeps beating repeatedly in my head
Like the surf against my thighs.
I sit in awe, moved beyond any human emotion
To see their souls bared so nakedly
Before my eyes.

I turn off the light of my fluorescent lamp
Seeking refuge on my bed.
But the naked souls continue to stare down at me
From the darkened ceiling, walls.
My mind moves with the shadows
Cast by the street lamp
Through my translucent pane.

Oh, but to have a magic wand instead of a red correction pen:

A magic wand to find a cure for cancer
That ravages Danny's mother and his total existence.
To take away that veil of confusion and fear
That occasionally sweeps across his face
And now across his page.

A magic wand to sober Jackie's father
So her eyes would not cloud with the memory
Of what was the evening last.
Her poems shout of anger, whisper of sadness
And of how life ought to be.

Oh, to be God or the Wizard of Oz:

To take the tears refusing to fall
From David's eyes,
Frightened and confused as he goes through divorce
With his mom and dad. To bring that mischief
Back into his once laughing eyes
So he can once again write of bikes and soccer
Instead of fear of a motherless world.

Oh, to be God:

To bottle cap that joy on Adam's face
As he writes of love and fun with such wit
They bring a chuckle to my throat.
And to desensitize Wendy's heart
So she can see beauty without a sense
Of loss and pain.

And for myself, a Tin Man transformation
For this hour of my day.
A Tin Man to stop me from feeling the brutal pain
And fears of each child whose poem I hold in my hand.
To step aside and merely correct and record
Each poem in my faded brown grading book.
Suddenly the room flashes with light.

A God? A wand? The Wizard of Oz?
Dare I dream of turning each soul
Into my own little Tin Man?
Dare I dream of depriving each child
Of his or her own right
To the joys and aches and pains
Of being alive?

Dare I try to stop the world that so painfully
Yet gloriously flows into these creative forms?
Dare I think of "poeming each out"
Even before each begins?

I gather the sheets
For tomorrow's class.
I, not God, not the Wizard of Oz,
But I, a mere human being
With all the frailties and strengths and pains and joys
Of each child whose work I hold in my hand.
I, I turn out the lights. ●

7 | EENY, MEENY, MINEY, MOE

Early one September morning in Hawai'i Kai, on the first day of school, a former third grader of mine, Destiny St. Laurent, waited in front of my classroom door with her younger brother, Philip. She greeted me with, "Miss Kakugawa, this is my brother Philip. He can't read or write and you're the only one who can help him. If he goes to fourth grade like this, he's going to be beaten up."

I looked at Philip who had his head down and I made a public proclamation. "Philip, you will not only learn to read and write but you are going to just love to read and write." He shook his head, saying, "No way, no way."

The following May, Destiny, a fifth grader then, approached me on the playground during my recess duty and said, "Miss Kakugawa, you really kept your promise to Philip and me." I said, " I did, didn't I?" Destiny said, "Yes, you did and thank you."

How did I keep my promise? The moment I promised Philip, "You will not only learn to read and write but you will love to read and write," I knew the first five minutes would be crucial and would determine the success or failure of his next nine months in third grade. I invited Philip into my classroom, picked up the third-grade basal reader and prayed. Students, no matter how clever their teachers' educational jargon, all know exactly how they're perceived by the textbooks their teachers use. I needed to use the third-grade basal reader because I sensed Philip knew exactly which books would be used for the third grade.

"Philip, do you know what this is?"

"Yes, that's the book for third grade."

"Right. I have a feeling you can already read from this book."

"No, I can't read. I wasn't even in the second grade book," meaning he wasn't able to read his second-grade reader. I took a deep breath, flipped through the reader and found a page with a lot of visual clues.

"Try this," I said and held my breath. He struggled, but using the context and visual clues, he was able to read one sentence. I stopped him with, "You just read from a third-grade book." Philip had perspiration dripping down from his nose and his body slumped in relaxation but his whole being signaled, "Whew, I can read a third-grade book."

Only in grades K-12 are there graded reading levels. We never speak of a 20-or a 40-year-old reading level. Philip was caught in this senseless rating system, believing he was less capable than his classmates.

I then discussed fear with him. "Philip, in my classroom, I don't want anyone to feel scared. You ever feel scared sometimes?" "All the time when the work is too hard." "In my class, no one needs to feel scared for long. When you think work is too hard or when I'm explaining something and you don't get it, there's no need to feel scared. Just tell me, 'I'm having trouble with this' and I will help you. Or tell me, 'I'm feeling scared' and we'll take care of it." "Okay." By then, the first day of school had begun for both of us.

In his first "published book" in October, he wrote, "I am special. You will like me because I am a good writer and a good reader." Sometime before December, he left the following note:

Thank you for teching me how to read. I thot I code never redd but you gave me the incaraging to read.
Love, Philip

P.S. I Bet you are married. (The word married was erased and correctly spelled by changing the y to an i)

Philip had assigned himself the task of having his teacher married that year. His end-of-the-year book contained the following page:

I thank my teacher for teaching me how to read and write. I love to read and I'm a good writer. I'm also very good in math.

How did Philip arrive at this state of mind? He was allowed to make his own decisions about his learning. I knew I could help him learn to read with storybooks but I also knew how Philip measured his own level of reading against the basal text. I showed him the basal text and a handful of storybooks. "Phil," I said, "I can help you read with this reader or with these storybooks. Which book do you want to use?" He chose the basal. A few weeks later he said, "Can I try the other books instead? This is too hard." He continued to keep his basal readers in his desk until June, perhaps to remind himself that he was like the other kids.

One day I said, "Phil, I am not able to give you all the help you need because I have the whole class to teach, but I can help you during recess or after school. Will you think about this and let me know?" I purposely didn't discuss this with his parents because I wanted Philip to be the decision maker. The next day he said, "Can you help me after school because I don't want to give up my recess?"

To help him with his writing, we began by reviewing what he knew about phonics, rhymes, consonants and vowel sounds and how every syllable usually has one or more vowels. We read for meaning in the storybooks.

For Philip's sake, I had discussed the role of a secretary in the business world and how the more successful an executive was, the more secretaries he had. It was a common sight to see Philip and other students working with their "secretaries," who were their fellow classmates, helping them with their reading and writing. We had quite a secretarial pool.

During the course of the term, Philip was later tested and qualified for special education classes. I spoke with the special education teacher and requested Philip be given a part in the decision to be in her class. The teacher provided the choice of two time slots. After I had explained how this teacher could give him more help than I could, he was allowed to visit her classroom. Later, he was given two choices: go to his special education class during his physical education and art period, or our writing workshop period. Although Philip loved soccer, PE and art, he chose to go during our PE and art time slot saying, "I don't want to miss writing in here." Importantly, Philip's parents were quietly behind him, respecting his decisions.

During the second semester, Philip told his special education teacher, "I'm not coming back anymore because I don't think you can help me anymore." The teacher, accepting that Philip was in control of his own learning, discussed this with me and then decided to introduce Philip to the computer. Philip then agreed to stay because we had no computers in our classroom.

Philip was now a confident young boy. For example, one day he offered the following: "Why don't you let me be your brains for you since you can't think of everything?" "Deal," I said. This was after a class function when he had asked if he could take a plate of cookies to our custodian and I had thanked him for his thoughtfulness, since I had not thought of it.

Philip contributed a lot to our social studies and science discussions. Students began to ask him, "How do you know so much about the Vikings?" Philip's answer was, "My sister reads to me," which once again supported my belief that a child's ability to learn is not dependent on his reading level. Being read to aloud cuts across all reading levels. Children ought not to be deprived of exposure to the benefit of good literature merely because they are not yet proficient readers.

I made it a practice to read to the class daily and explored all the literary devices that authors use. Creative drama also became an integral part of exploring literary works. Children became the characters, dramatized plots from beginning to end, created settings with their bodies, and used spontaneous dialog to interpret and recreate the authors' work. Philip and his classmates came to know how a piece of good literature was crafted. His writing began to speak of characters with distinct personalities, to rise to climaxes, have recognizable plots and have discernable endings.

In essence, all the language arts skills required in third grade were being taught throughout the entire curriculum and not confined to language arts. This included reading, writing and oral communications skills. I incorporated all the skills spelled out in the teacher's manual of the basal text reading program, thus fulfilling the third-grade requirement with my own teaching. However, I covered these skills without using the basal readers themselves, because there were other means to the same ends which engaged the children in more interesting and creative activities.

What happened to Philip as told by his mother, Miki St. Laurent:

School for Phil was very painful. But… he SURVIVED! Helping him at various stages in his life were some caring people. One of them was Frances Kakugawa who was Phil's third-grade teacher. He entered her room, a student who was being tested for the need for special services for the second time in his life. Although he showed signs of reading difficulty as early as kindergarten, he was tested in first grade and did not meet the two-year discrepancy criteria so he did not qualify to receive any extra help. The State Department of Education policy at that time stated that a student had to wait two years before being tested again so Phil had to wait until he was in third grade. By this time, he showed a four-year discrepancy.

As his parents, we watched Phil's self-esteem drain from his SOUL year after year and as his mother and a teacher, I tried to teach him at home. Phil, however, felt he was being punished. After completing an entire day at school, he viewed my help at home as "more school." Needless to say, I felt frustrated and helpless. But Frances was there to help.

Frances made every one of her students feel "special" and Phil was no exception. She accomplished this by having them write about their feelings, their experiences, their dreams, their fears, their every thought and bind them into little books. One of Phil's first books was titled I Am Special! *That year, he wrote several books under Frances's guidance and at the end of the year Phil and the rest of his classmates celebrated an anthology of poetry at an Author's Tea, with parents and school dignitaries in attendance. The day of the tea was a very special one for Phil. Not only was it his birthday, but he was given the opportunity to recite his poems as an author.*

As Phil pressed on through school, he continued to struggle with his reading and writing. We began to understand more about his learning styles after he was diagnosed with dyslexia. Phil is an auditory learner who thrives in a "hands-on" learning environment. He also has short-term memory problems which means he is able to focus on only one task at a time. As a consequence, if his brain is focusing on listening to the teacher, he is not able to write at the same time because it would mean his brain has to focus on forming the letters to write his notes. And using a tape recorder was only useful if he remembered to turn it on.

Throughout secondary school, the work became more difficult and I wanted to let the world know that no matter how hard Phil tried, he was caught in a system that "wasn't flexible enough to meet his needs." Instead, he had to adapt to the only way the system was accustomed to handling such students. It didn't matter if it took him five times longer to do an assignment than it would an average stu-

dent. He simply had to do it, even if it meant pulling him out of the one thing he was good in, sports. It also didn't matter that he would do better sitting near the front of the room, but his last name began with S and students were seated alphabetically. He was content in sitting in the back of the room where he was barely noticeable until we requested he be moved to the front. It didn't matter further that he would do best if the assignments were written down for him on a piece of paper instead of having them on a board to be copied by the students before leaving class, given that Phil's brain was consumed at that moment with packing his bag and moving on to the next class. Because it didn't matter to most but the few caring people he had throughout his 13 years of school, Phil operated in survivor mode and our goal for him was to "just finish school so we can get on with life."

The turning point for me came with the realization I had to stop being the teacher-mom and start becoming solely the mom, because our relationship became very strained. It wasn't until he entered college when something as simple as having access to another student's notes for the class he was taking, made all the difference in the world to him. He could focus on what the professor was saying and later look at the notes as needed. That semester proved to be a turning point in Phil's life. Feeling confident and desiring to forge ahead without any help, Phil finally found a system that worked for him.

Today, after graduating from college, Phil is not just a survivor, he is, in addition, an electrician and a productive citizen with a caring and compassionate heart. When asked about Ms. Kakugawa, he simply smiles and says, "She was patient AND pushy … BUT in a good way." As for me, I am not just a mom of a survivor, but the proud mom of a beautiful human being.

There are many more Philips with special needs in every classroom. Allowing and encouraging students to take charge of their own learning brings a sense of peace and builds confidence within all. Gary, another third grader, attended special education and occupational therapy classes most of the day. When he entered our classroom, he spoke in short phrases and I had difficulty understanding half of what he said. For two weeks he did nothing in class, not even hold a pencil. I knew this situation couldn't continue so one day I took him out of class and said, "Gary, you are not doing any work in this class." Before I could continue, he interrupted me with, "This my class. I was in second grade before. This my class." "Yes," I said, "This is your class." He was reminding me that I was not to threaten him. His message stopped me from saying, "If you don't do the work in here, maybe you don't belong in third grade." Clearly he was wiser than I was.

He showed his first sign of interest by asking, "Why is everyone writing like that and I'm not?" He was pointing to the chalkboard where cursive writing was being introduced. "Gary," I explained, "that's because I decided that you're not quite ready for cursive writing until your hands get stronger."

"No," he retorted, "I can. Teach me, Miss Kakugawa, teach me." "Okay," I said and introduced him to cursive writing. After a few attempts, he said, "You're right. I'm not ready yet," and returned to dictating his writing to his private "secretary." Clearly, Gary was at peace with himself after being allowed to have a chance to learn to write cursively, and although he failed, he knew he had a great deal to say about his own education.

Declaring, "I want to write a book, too," led Gary to write his first book. His mother gathered photos of birds taken by his grandfather, who was visiting from China. Gary dictated a story for each photo, which was duly transcribed by his "teacher secretary." He joined us at our Authors' Tea. His page on the author's page read:

This is the first book that this author has made. The author learns things from his teacher and from the students. The author likes to write.

Gary's second book had as its topic, a collection of Norman Rockwell's paintings. One day I watched *Breaking Ties*, a television show about Rockwell, starring Jason Robards. While taking a shower the following weekend, it came to me how I could help Gary with his writing. I took my book of Rockwell paintings, which had no text, and asked Gary to select his favorite ones. He word-attacked the title saying slowly, "Nor-man Rock-well. Who is Norman Rockwell?" I told him who he was and then sent him to his desk with stickers to mark his selections. He returned chuckling and said, "Look, Norman Rockwell is painting his own picture!"

After school I saw a whole lot of yellow stickers on the book and thought, "Oh no, he selected every page," but I was wrong. I was very curious to know why he had selected the ones he did. The next day I sat with Gary and said, "Choose one of your pictures and write a story about it." He grimaced over one particular painting so I asked, "Why didn't you choose this?"

He said, "I don't like old people. This one has old people."

I teased him with," Oh Gary, how about me? Aren't I old?" "No," he said. "No, you're not old."

His first selection was the painting, "Thanksgiving". He wrote, "The son came home from the Air Force." He spelled each word correctly, but wanted help with Force. I asked him, "How do you know he's in the Air Force?" He pointed to the AF insignia on the uniform and said, "I know that stands for Air Force." This was a perfect example of demonstrated reading comprehension, something that teachers need to be aware of.

After writing stories for three additional paintings, he checked the spelling of the name of each painting by turning the page over where each title was printed on the back. This was a good example showing he was, in a sense, teaching himself editing skills. His page on the author's page read: "This is the author's second book. The author likes to write."

One day I asked him, "How do you feel about school? I push you a lot by saying, 'Gary, you must do your math. Gary, do your writing.' Do you feel angry at me sometimes?" He looked at me in shock and practically shouted, "Angry at you? No!" He sang and hummed a lot in class while he worked. Sometimes this noise rose to such a disturbing level that I had to ask him to work quietly. What a shame, I thought, for I knew how happy he was. This behavior represented such a change from his constant grunts in September.

Gary was constantly at my side asking, "Why, why, why?" I accorded him a lot of attention, yet didn't worry about how this would bother the class. I felt a tug at my heart when a group of his peers approached me with a chuckle and said, "You and Gary are like Charlotte and Wilbur." referring to the book, *Charlotte's Web*. Once again, I had received compassion and understanding from my students, and instead of resenting Gary for demanding so much of my time, they watched in amusement. Gary, in turn, reciprocated his peers' love and compassion for him. One day, his mother complained about how one of Gary's classmates had pushed him into a puddle. Gary quickly countered his mother and said, "It was an accident; we were playing."

He also learned to behave in socially acceptable ways among his peers. In September, for example, he would place his hand on his rectum and say, "Doo doo, doo doo. Where bathroom?" However, in time, he learned to rise above this level of communication. In September, he took 45 minutes to write his name and had no eye contact with anyone, and he would build houses with his notebooks instead of writing in them. By June, he was a socially accepted member of our class, performing at his own level of competence with considerable dignity and self-confidence.

One of Gary's constant questions concerned my mother and where she lived. At the time, my mother lived on the Big Island. That Christmas, Gary was planning to visit his grandparents on the Big Island, so I arranged to take him out to lunch and to visit my mother. He entered her house and quickly walked through every room, asking many questions. He answered all the questions posed by my mother and later walked in the backyard to pick tangerines. He then wanted to see where my oldest brother lived, so I drove him to my brother's house. Throughout the rest of the year, Gary would whisper to me, "That was good, yeah? Going to McDonald's, just the two of us having lunch together in Hilo and me naming all the names of my classmates." Gary was the only student I've had who would elbow me in my ribs saying, "Teach me, Miss Kakugawa, teach me."

Choices should not be made lightly, as they can affect many aspects of a person's life. Spence, for example, was not a reader, although he knew how to read. He avoided books like the plague. So with my ice pick in my hand, I began chipping away to get to the source of his reading problem. Without knowing the source, how was I expected to help him? I "talked story" with Spence a lot: in the lunch line, walking to the library and during my recess duty days. From these sessions, I discovered that his parents took him to the library every two weeks and he had a grand passion for sports.

I chipped even more by deciding to call his parents for a conference and what I discovered was two very devoted parents who wanted the best for their only child. I sensed some insecurities in their roles as parents. I discussed with them my specific concern with Spence's hatred of books. After more chipping, I learned that Spence's home environment offered almost no opportunities for decision-making.

For example, when he went to the library, his mother

selected all his books for him. His mother picked out his clothes in the morning and when they dined out, Spence's parents chose his food for him to ensure good nutrition for their son. I came to the conclusion that the source of Spence's problem in reading was not reading related. What he needed was to be respected, trusted and allowed to make many of his own decisions.

Working with his parents, I charted out our first plan of action. Spence would be allowed to select his own books at the library. His parents expressed their concern by asking, "But what if he chooses only simple books?" I assured them that this was quite acceptable, since what we wanted to achieve was to allow Spence to make his own selections. He could test his new freedom by selecting simple books if he wanted and that, too, would be acceptable. In addition, Spence would also select his own clothes in the morning.

They showed their concern with, "But what if his clothes do not match?" I assured them that if he wore a polka dot shirt with plaid pants, his choice would not demean any parenting skills, and what was important here was that they needed to trust Spence. I shared a letter I had once received from a mother of a five-year-old: "Please do not think I'm an unfit mother, but my daughter won't leave the house without her summer sundress today." I pointed out that this incident happened on a rainy and very cold morning in December, making the point that the important thing was the child's decision-making process, not her choice of a particular dress.

Spence's parents and I met once a month. Happily, Spence was gradually making more decisions for himself while his parents were becoming more comfortable in their roles. Still, Spence's passion for sports was not being nurtured because his parents felt he needed to read non-sports books; they regarded sports as being not very academic. I suggested, and his parents agreed, he could read *Sports Illustrated* as well as the sports page in the daily newspapers as part of his reading material.

By June, Spence was not only reading with enjoyment but he was an active member of his family. On the last day of school, Spence came to me with, "I don't want school to end. I learned to love books but what if during the summer I come to hate books again?" I asked him if he would like a summer reading contract and he happily agreed. We signed an agreement specifying that he would read 12 books of his choice during the summer. He would also write a response to each book. Then, if he fulfilled his contract, I would take him out to lunch; if not, he would take me out to lunch.

On the last day of summer, I happily took Spence out to lunch. For his part, he had a flower lei for me. His love of sports was obvious because all the book titles were related to sports. The following year, he returned to me after the fourth grade for a summer contract. This time his contract read, "For every three sports books, I will read a book on another subject." He agreed, signed and fulfilled his contract.

After his fifth-grade year, his contract included some book titles I had recommended. Spence returned every year throughout his middle school years and I continued to take him out to lunch. When he graduated from high school we celebrated over lunch. He sent me a note that said, "Because of you, I am a reader today. I cannot thank you enough." He graduated from college this year. It was time to put my ice pick away.

Spence and his parents taught me an invaluable lesson. The source of a reading or any other problem may be found somewhere other than what might be expected and sometimes, a bit of detective work is needed to discover its source.

When students became aware that I was making decisions about their own learning, they began to get very suspicious and, like Gary, started to elbow me in less painful and physical ways. During one February morning, I was discussing alliteration. Wendy looked at me and said, "My first book in October, *The Whirling Wind* by Wendy Weaver, had alliteration in my title. Did you know that?" When she heard my yes, she said, "Then why didn't you teach me about alliteration then?" I honestly confessed, "Wendy, I didn't think you were ready to learn about alliteration in October."

Later, Wendy came to me and privately asked, "Miss Kakugawa, can you teach me everything you know?" I answered, "I would not be able to do that because sometimes a person has to be at a different level of maturity to understand certain things. But," I went on, "I will try to answer all of your questions." Years later, at her wedding shower, I wrote and read a poem with a confession that in actuality, that was all I knew during her third-grade year with me, and that I had taught her all I knew.

Wendy was a very demanding student and tested me one day when she came to me during recess with an entourage of students behind her. She asked rather defiantly, "Miss Kakugawa, is there a Santa Claus?" I knew from the look on her face that she needed a yes from me. "Yes, there is a Santa Claus for me because I believe in him. Do you believe in Santa Claus? If you do, then there is a Santa Claus for you." Wendy turned around and said, "See? What did I tell you?" And she walked away.

My heart ached one Christmas when a mother of a former first-grade student of mine, whom I had taught in Jackson, Michigan, asked in her Christmas letter to me that I write to her daughter. My former pupil had lost a son in a car accident and had lost custody of her two other children. Her mother explained, "We are poor folks and we couldn't afford any good lawyer for Lorna. I know you can help her if she heard from you." I wished I had, at that moment, a magic wand to help Lorna as I had helped her in our first-grade class years ago. I was humbled to think I was still being asked, "Teach me; help me. Help me make some decisions." This incident speaks to the responsibilities that teachers carry.

Anna, in third grade, asked me to teach her Shakespeare after I had used *Witches' Brew* in a poetry choral reading. "Teach me about *Macbeth*," she demanded. I asked her to have lunch with me in our classroom and during this time, I told her the synopsis of *Macbeth*. The grapevine went into overtime that year as I began to have more and more lunches in our classroom with individual students who had requested Shakespeare. I must have oversold myself when I had introduced *Witches' Brew* with, "Since you're such an intelligent bunch, I'm going to introduce you to Shakespeare, whose work is usually taught in high school."

The highlight of my Shakespearean efforts came one afternoon when a parent shared the following with me: Her son asked at the dinner table one night, "Would anyone care to hear Shakespeare?" Then he proceeded to recite *Witches' Brew* by heart.

When students observe they are trusted to use their intelligence wisely, it frequently enables them to make decisions for their own learning, and the classroom then becomes a place for a peaceful, comfortable and natural existence. When they discover their teachers are simultaneously making informed decisions about their own learning, this promotes a state of active learning for all.

Jennifer, a brilliant student, was in a math group of one because she was able to read, analyze and work on her math book by herself. I checked her work daily and held a conference with her once a week. Other students approached me with, "Can I work on my math like Jennifer?"

"Of course!" I replied. "There are certain things you need to do. You will need to figure out the problems by yourself by reading the book and be able to handle the additional work at the end of the chapter. If you have two or more errors, and you're not able to self-correct, you will have to return to one of our two math groups."

These students, when given the same privileges as Jennifer, would happily work on their own and when they encountered difficulty, would say, "I guess I need help. May I work with you in the math group instead?"

Thus Jennifer was able to continue with her work without any feelings of animosity from her peers, but rather respect for her ability because they, too, had been accorded the same privileges.

Ryan was an avid reader and I would often find him trying to read one of his books by hiding it under his desk during social studies or science. I arrived at the following solution: "Ryan, there is no need to hide your reading from me. How about a deal? If you can read and listen and handle two things at one time, that will be OK. If you prove that you can't do both, then you'll have to put your books away." Delighted with this response, Ryan openly read his books, but gradually he put them away. To me, this was an example that there is no enemy in the classroom — that is, the teacher — when the teaching and learning environment is based on mutual respect and trust and students are not under the total control of an adult.

Philip M. in Hilo, a first grader, took full advantage of this trust. I had introduced haiku poetry to the class with, "If during any time of the day, you feel inspired to write a haiku poem, feel free to do so, either in this classroom or under a tree. Just be sure to tell me if you're going outside." Philip could often be seen under a tree during math time, working on his poetry. Teachers would often come to report to me that one of my students was outside and did I know that? "Yes," was my response. "I know."

Two other youngsters, Cy and Miki, confirmed my belief that children, no matter what age, are quite capable of making appropriate decisions and resolving problems if given the opportunity without adult interference. I invited my three-year-old grandnephew, Cy, his mother, Jill, and seven-year-old Jacy out to breakfast at the Hilo Hawaiian Hotel. When the menus arrived I said, "Order whatever you want. The treat is on me."

When the waitress arrived to take our orders, Cy pointed to the picture of a banana split. The waitress looked at me and asked, "What is he having?" I turned to Cy and asked," Did you tell her your order?" He pointed to the banana split and said, "Banana split." The waitress, probably thinking she needed to ask the other mature person at the table since the oldest one didn't seem to be very responsible, turned to Jill. Jill said, "Cy, did you order?"

When the waitress brought our orders, she placed the banana split in front of Cy, stood there for awhile and said, "I guess this makes sense. There's milk in ice cream and fruit in bananas." Then she walked away.

A few weeks later, Cy and his family were invited to breakfast by another aunt and two younger cousins. Cy looked over the menu and whispered to his mother, "I better not order a banana split because Joshua and Zachary will not eat their breakfast if they see my banana split." Then he ordered waffles.

How often do we give children choices with a hidden decision already made? Had Jill and I negated Cy's choice that first morning he ordered a banana split, our message would have been, "Cy, you are not able to make right choices. We know what is best for you. You cannot be trusted, not yet." And after we take away his confidence and condition him to look to others for approval, will we wonder later why Cy lacks confidence and is inept when it comes to taking risks and making appropriate choices and decisions?

Cy not only learned to select his own breakfast without adult censorship, but he was able to analyze and make an appropriate decision by himself a few weeks later when he ordered waffles in the presence of his younger cousins. Did knowing he had the freedom to choose make it possible for Cy to deny himself a banana split that morning?

Another special friend of mine, six-year-old Miki Lee, was with me one day in a shoe department. After trying on a new pair of shoes, I put on my own pair of boots and was about to tie the laces when Miki quickly asked, "Can I do that?" My first inclination was to show her how to lace my boots — how to cross the laces so they would be properly laced. Luckily I stopped and simply said, "Sure. When you get done, the laces will have to be crossed like this," and I showed her how I wanted them to look. She started with my left boot. It took her five to eight minutes to lace my left boot while I sat and people-watched. Then she laced my right boot. Both boots were laced perfectly. The entire process had taken more than 10 minutes.

When I arrived home and began to unlace my boots, a big smile formed not only on my face but inside of me as well. The left boot was laced in the most intricate way with the laces twisted and entangled in various ways beneath the crosses. The right boot, on the other hand, was laced as I would have done it. I had but one thought: Thank goodness I didn't insult Miki by telling her how to do it. She had experimented and through her own explorations, had learned to lace a pair of boots. By being silent, I had given her permission to experiment; I had not undermined that feeling of "I can do it."

Experiences with Cy and Miki make me reflect on how children learn things like self-confidence, making good choices and love of experimentation. Would classroom lessons on "learning to make good choices" or "learning how to experiment" develop the ability to make appropriate choices or the desire to explore and experiment? Would lectures, films and programs filled with activities and strategies help develop self-confidence and the ability to make appropriate choices when teenagers are confronted with drugs, alcohol and sex? Or, are such things as attitudes, motivation and self-confidence gained as a result of how others respond to children's attempts in every-day, mundane situations like choosing their meals in restaurants or trying out something on the spur of the moment?

How often do children learn something about themselves and about the world from how we respond to their initiatives? Are we aware that as we react to our children in those little seemingly unimportant everyday-life situations, we are teaching them either to be self-confident or to look toward others for guidance, either to take risks or to be passive, fearing failure? Philip, Gary, Spence and their peers were able to explore their capabilities because they were in an environment that said, "Yes, you can," with teaching and learning strategies custom-fitted to their strengths and learning styles.

Yes, I Will

When he takes my hand in his,
His tiny little fingers curled around mine,
I am filled with a great sense of duty,
Duty to keep this world
Free from fear and evil.
When I feel his hand in mine,
The contrast: spring to autumn,
I feel compelled to live
Every minute of my life
With love and human kindness
So this world that belongs to him
Will be a place where his deepest secrets
Will be safe,
Where all his dreams and hopes

Become possibilities,
And this world becomes
The greatest, most trusted friend,
Anyone could ever have.
Oh, I will live so I can make
All the difference in his life,
For having trusted his hand in mine.

Frances H. Kakugawa 🍎

8 | TEACHER, TEACHER, YOU'RE TURNING BLACK!

"Our young must be taught that racial peculiarities do exist, but that beneath the skin, beyond the differing features and into the true heart of being, fundamentally we are more alike, my friend, than we are unalike."

Maya Angelou
Wouldn't Take Nothing for my Journey Now

"Teacher, teacher, you're turning black! Oh my God, you're turning black!" Seven-year-old Keisha's face showed total panic as she greeted me one morning when I entered her classroom, a resource writing teacher. Puzzled, I asked her, "Black? Where?" She pointed to my legs and said, "There! Oh my God, you're turning black!"

"Keisha," I explained. "I'm wearing black stockings." Still frightened, she touched my legs and asked, "Why do you want to be black?" I took a model's stance and said, "Because black stockings make me feel beautiful and chic." Then I held my skirt and slowly did a pirouette. She walked away with, "Why would anyone want to be black?" I silently thought, *Oh Keisha, is it that hard being black?* It is.

In my sixth-grade class of children of military men and women we were discussing racial prejudice. The students of varied racial backgrounds were sharing their experiences. All, that is, except the African-American students. They sat quietly, shook their heads and said, "You wouldn't want to know." I sensed they were still suffering from the hurt and indignities of being treated as less than human beings.

Sometimes, being rather oblivious to color and race has merits. I had spent the previous evening watching the Miss America contest. I noticed that the winner had the same surname as one of my students so when Yolanda entered our classroom the following morning, I greeted her with, "Hey, Yolanda! Did you watch the Miss America contest last night? Are you related to her?" Yolanda shook her head with an amused look on her face and said, "Miss Kakugawa!"

"No," I pursued, "I'm serious. You have the same last name." She chuckled, shook her head and repeated, "Miss Kakugawa!" as if I were a complete idiot. Then I realized the newly crowned Miss America was white and Yolanda was African-American. I did feel like an idiot, but a pleased idiot. I liked myself all day because I discovered I was color-blind and Yolanda had also made this discovery of her teacher.

One morning, the counselor brought a new student to our sixth-grade classroom. An African-American couple stood there with their son who was fighting back tears. I put my arms around him and said, "I know, the first day can be hard but I'll help you, so why don't you come in." His father looked at his wife, then at me and said, "Son, you're going to be all right. You got a good teacher." And I walked into the classroom with my arms around our new student, John.

Later, John and I discussed his first day of school and he said I was the first teacher who had touched him in an accepting way. What a blessing that I could, in a few seconds, let John and his parents know my private and professional beliefs and practices through a simple gesture. I wonder how teachers today communicate with their students when they are cautioned against human touch lest they be accused of sexual overtones. My male teaching partner that year occasionally told me, "You're so lucky you're female. I can't show affection toward my students because I'm male. Sometimes I want to comfort them by putting my arms around them but I'm afraid." During all the years of my teaching career, it was a habit of mine to stand by the door and hug each child as he or she left for the day. It brought a peaceful closure, no matter what the day was like for both of us. Some of the sixth graders who were taller than me, would settle for a handshake but this was rare. They were still children needing hugs.

At one school, my students came from military backgrounds because one or both of their parents were in the armed forces, so they had traveled extensively. I added their experiences to our curriculum. I dropped our social studies text and had the class work on an international theme. The students had to do research on a country of their choice and prepare a project. The culmination would be an International Luncheon. On that day, students would bring dishes representative of their research country. Parents were invited, and we sang international songs, shared our projects and lunched on various cultural cuisine. The purpose of this project was to have students develop their research skills by tapping into their own real-life experiences and to bring about cultural and human understanding.

One year, I did not offer Jake the option of choosing which country to study. In his daily journal, I discovered his hatred for the Japanese. As December 7 neared, his reference to those "Japs" would appear more and more. "I hate those Japs" jolted me no matter how many times I read it. His grandfather had been at Pearl Harbor when it was bombed by the Japanese. His father shared his grandfather's feelings toward that event.

It was time to work on our social studies project so I told Jake, "Jake, I would like you to do your research on Japan." He said, "But I don't like those people. I hate them." I said, "I know, Jake. But you know what they say — sometimes you can weaken your enemy by getting to know how they feel and think."

He accepted that. At this point, I knew that my use of the word "enemy" and my recognition of his feelings toward the "Japs" helped him to say yes. As he worked on his research, his journal entries began to show changes in his attitude. "I no longer hate the Japanese" made me want to do cartwheels. No more "Japs." At one point he said, "Miss Kakugawa, I wish I knew a Japanese I could interview." I looked at him and said, "Interview me." He said, "You?" During our interview, he discovered that both my parents would never hear from their families in Hiroshima after the use of the first atomic bomb. At the end, his conclusion read, "I no longer hate the Japanese people. I discovered that we are very much alike." At the luncheon, his mother had helped him with his research by preparing a Japanese dish. Jake will never know how my skin had crawled each time I had read "Jap" in his journal. Nor will he ever know how, as a child, I had walked to school with my head down during the war because of the "Hey, Jap" thrown at me simply because the enemy had worn my face on December 7, 1941.

I could not help but be pleased with my intuitive actions, for considering the context into which my plans were placed. Had I not intervened with Jake, he would not have selected Japan. We both would have been deprived of a rich experience had I left Jake alone with his feelings of hating the "Japs." When I intervened and tried to talk him into researching the Japanese, I gave no lecture about how he needed to change his attitude. Instead, I had used the word "enemy," which was how he perceived the Japanese. Throughout his research, he naturally and internally replaced old attitudes, feelings and perceptions. Throughout the entire process, he was not placed in a position where he was being judged.

The bottom line, I feel, is the subjective direction his research took — the use of human resources. Had he worked with textbook knowledge alone, I am not sure he would have seen the "Japs" as Japanese. Imagine discovering his sixth-grade teacher was one of those "Japs!"

The classroom, although physically enclosed within four walls, extends to each student's family and community, and often a child will lead them. In my first-grade class at Jackson, Michigan, my students were all Caucasian. I began to hear racial references in their daily conversations that displayed ignorance. How do you break through this ignorance of racial prejudice in six-year-olds? I told them the story of *The Boy With Green Hair*. For an entire day, those children who had blond hair would be treated differently from those who didn't, merely because of the color of their hair. They had to be last in line because they were blond. They did all the chores in the classroom. Before the day was over, I could sense genuine anger in these children. These children wanted other students to experience being discriminated against so we did. We explored this further with our own history of discrimination and how this was not fiction.

Weeks later, a student's mother visited me after school. She warned me that her own mother was planning to see me and when she did I was not to take her seriously. Evidently, my student Mary's grandmother had used the word "nigger" in reference to someone and Mary had sat her grandmother down to tell her the story of *The Boy With Green Hair*. Grandmother was upset with what Mary was learning in my classroom. Mary's mother said she and her husband learned something important from Mary as they, too, have been so careless.

These students renewed my faith in why I was there, that education will and can change attitudes and behavior in and beyond our classrooms. Once again, it was that age-old process of having classroom context determine the direction of our best-laid plans. Our paper curriculum becomes alive only with the students making the final decisions and students becoming the determining factors in keeping it real, meaningful and alive. And most important, to allow ourselves to respect each student with dignity and love and to allow each of them to learn through our own modeling. We adults have had problems in creating racial harmony in our lives. Perhaps we need to turn to our children as I have to five-year-old Alan. Following is an open letter I wrote to him.

Dear Alan,

You were in kindergarten when we met. I walked out of that airplane on a hot blistering day and as I anxiously scanned the terminal, I saw you, a serious little boy with a bunch of gladiolus in his arms. I recognized you from the snapshot your mother had sent me. You quickly came to me and said in a very adult manner, "Aloha, Frances." I thanked you and remember putting my hand on your shoulder for a brief moment. Then I walked to where your mother stood.

Your mother and I were meeting for the first time. We were no strangers, really. We have been pen pals since the seventh grade. We practically grew up together, your mother and I, although miles apart.

I had left Hawai'i about 10 hours previously and now I was in Michigan. A wonderful year began the moment you put the freshly cut gladiolus in my arms. I lived with you and your family for an entire school year while I taught first graders nearby. We shared and learned all year long.

Remember how you'd come up to my room and say, "Can I play your ukulele?" and how you'd strum "Twinkle Twinkle Little Star?" Remember that day it snowed and how I had rushed out in my nightgown because that was the first time I had seen snow? You stood and looked at me as though I were the silliest grown-up you had ever seen.

I still see your serious brown eyes and that little frown on your forehead as you bombarded me with questions about Hawai'i. I had to be careful because I felt you'd remember every story you heard about Hawai'i. You were a good sport. I remember the evening your eyes filled with tears as you swallowed the barbecued octopus at the dinner table. You never refused the many strange dishes I prepared. No, you gamely tried them all. You were the first to use chopsticks without dropping half the dinner on the floor.

Surely you remember the many baths I gave you and the songs we'd sing as I soaped you. It was in May, a month before I was to leave that you told me something very special. You were covered with soapsuds in the bathtub when you very quietly said, "Frances, you don't look different anymore."

I quietly asked you, "How do I look?" and you very matter-of-factly said, "You look like Frances." You look like Frances. So you grew and learned along with the rest of us. Your mother had laughed at me when I had written, "I'm Japanese. Won't I create problems for you in your neighborhood?"

I have thought of that night often, Alan, and wonder, can all of our prejudices and displays of fear and hate be eliminated with a better understanding and knowledge of each other? Should we keep our first impressions of strange people and their customs and appearances to ourselves until they no longer appear strange? Should we refrain from saying, "You're different from me" until the day we are able to say, "You're like the rest of us?"

Love, Frances

P.S. I have since learned that the reason why your family and I never visited your grandma's home that year was because she did not welcome me in her home because of my racial background. And your family had refused to accept any invitation that was not extended to me.

Since 1999, Alan and I have had numerous dinners together during his business trips to Hawai'i.

| **DEAREST JOURNAL**

A Stranger Among Us

Three young lads walk the mall,
Passing my book signing at Waldenbooks.
One lad breaks away,
After turning his head
Toward the book display
On a tripod near me.

"What kind of book is this?
Did you write this?"

"Yes," I say, to the lad,
Wearing a tiny hoop in one lobe,
A silver stud in his nose.
"This is a book of poems on caregiving." *

"I write poems, too. I set them to music,
Do you want to hear one of my poems?"

He rapped his poem in perfect rhythm,
Musical rhymes, poignantly searching
For the meaning of life.

I open my book to offer him
My simple poem, "A Poet's Declaration."

* *Mosaic Moon: Caregiving Through Poetry*

He reads it, looks at me and says,
"You're the first person who understands me."

We talk of how it is
To be a poet ...
The aloneness, the pain, the joy.

"No one knows me as you do."
He hands me Mosaic Moon,
I sign it To Jason.

"Dammit," I think, after he leaves
To join his two companions
With my book in his hand ...
"How can one poem from a stranger
Help him feel there is someone after all,
Who knows and understands him?
How did he recently leave
Thirteen years of school behind him,
A lonely stranger ...

Frances H. Kakugawa

My classroom would have been a very lonely place without journal writing. Journal writing became a means to develop a very personal relationship with each individual student. With out this intimate relationship, my students and I would have remained strangers — and can you imagine spending nine months among strangers? At least at cocktail parties you'd be given something other than a piece of chalk to hold in your useless hands.

I had two specific types of relationships with my students and both began on the first day of school. One was a group relationship, where I saw the students as a whole. It was based on classroom rules developed by the class, which spoke to grade level expectations and on mutual group respect, trust and dignity.

But it was the other relationship that made waking up every morning a joyous event because in a class of 30, there would be 30 individual relationships nurtured and developed on a very intimate and professional level. How and where did we begin? Certain rules were introduced with the first journal entry on the opening day of school:

1. This journal is between you and me. No one can read your journal without your permission, including your parents and teacher.

2. If you wish to keep anything in your journal private from me, fold your sheet and write "Private" on it and I will respect your wishes.

Inevitably, no matter at what grade level, a few students would test the privacy privilege by writing "Private" on their entries, but eventually they'd disclose their entries to me when they learned that by concealing their entries, they would not receive any responses. This privacy clause meant a lot to the students during parent-teacher conferences when parents who are denied access to their children's journals, graciously and respectfully ask their children for permission to read them, then abide by their children's answers. I often wondered whether these parents could hear what was so loudly expressed by their children's faces: Wow! Adults are respecting my privacy.

This relationship that I sought did not come overnight,

but as with most genuine relationships, evolved over time based on mutual respect and trust. Students' journals were read daily during morning recesses except on those days when I was on recess duty; these I read during my lunchtime. Knowing that I read their journals during morning recesses, my students expected to read my responses as soon as the morning recess ended. Many would go straight to the journal shelf; many would give me a private look and smile after reading what I had written, while others wore a knowing look, or a grin, without exchanging a look with me. One of the first inquiries on Monday mornings was, "Are you on duty this week?"

Many journals began as daily logs of activities, where, day after day, I would read what students did after school up to bedtime. Soon I would receive, "Why do you write so much in Ann's journal and so little in mine?" My honest response: "Well, Ann writes of things I can respond to. Try it … when you write of what you do every day after school, I find there's really nothing for me to say. Do write of how you honestly feel and think about things that matter to you." This tack helps these students to delve deeper into their lives instead of repetitiously reporting routine, daily events.

Here is an exchange I had with one sixth-grade student:

2-16
Dear Journal,
How do you think up all of your answers to my journal? Do you take them out of a book, or do you just think them up as you go along on how you feel? You have a very creative mind. You can think of anything. I wish I would be as talented as you.
Leann

My response: *Because I'm almost as smart as you. Thanks for the compliments. I just take them out of my left pocket.*

2-17

Dear Journal,

Nonsense! I won't be as smart as you for a long time. Meanwhile, I'm still learning. You're out of school except for being a teacher. I could never run a class like ours. I could never write poetry as good as you. I'm just not sensitive as you are. Besides, I can't even write poetry.

Leann

My response: *Anyone who can analyze me as you have shows intelligence. Hey, maybe we both should form a mutual admiration Fan Club!!!*

Denise was less complimentary in her remarks:

OK. On Tuesday I was not very pleased to see an OK for my response! Everybody likes to read something nice. And it's disappointing to find a "OK. Good, Nice." We like to read other things than those! Do you think you can cease these "OK, Good, and Nice?" If you can we all will be very pleased.

Thank you (only if you do)

Denise

My response: *I write when I have something interesting to respond to. Sometimes I feel there's nothing to say. So, my dear one, how about some insightful, exciting, fantastic journal entries?*

As I got to know my students I could match my responses to their sense of humor, their poetic souls or to their serious and no-nonsense selves, and I sometimes even succeeded in drawing them out of their humorless, unimaginative selves with my gentle prodding. And addresses such as "my friend" or "my dear" often let me in gently without too negative an impact.

Ryan, a third grader, had a sense of humor to match almost any adult, so I tried to get him to write in more detail:

Hey, what is this? Reading for the Bored? This will bore any reader to death. I want to know you! Yawn … yawn … yawn … good night.

If I wanted students to be honest, I, too, had to be prepared to accept and deal with this honesty. One day I read the following after disciplining a sixth grader:

I hate you Ms. Kakugawa.

After swallowing my initial shock and discomfort, I responded with: *I understand why you feel this way. I hope you'll be able to see the cause of the problem we discussed. I'm glad you can be so honest with me, Tod.* A few days later I found the following note on my desk with a red-colored heart:

Dear Ms. Kakugawa,
I appreciate you very much. You've helped me a lot and care for me a lot and I'd like to say, I love you very much.
Tod

Journal writing allowed me to enter into the thoughts and feelings of certain students which then gave me the opportunity to counsel and help them and enhance their problem-solving process. Following are selected excerpts from Melody's journal on shyness:

11-4
Dear Journal,
The real me that lies inside my body is a very nice girl. It is

very shy. It wants to speak up but it's afraid to let anything out. I'll tell it to speak up because people don't like a person who can't speak up about anything.

My response: *I'm sure you'll speak up after you feel comfortable with us. Just do it! The longer you wait, the harder it gets.*

11-16
Dear Journal,
    I wish I wasn't so shy. I talk a lot at home but I hardly say anything at school. Maybe I don't talk at school because I'm not used to other people. I'm going to try to talk a lot more even if it kills me. I don't think it will kill me but I just wrote that because I hear a lot of people saying that.

My response: *I'll help you. And I'll call the doctor if it kills you. Kidding, of course.*

11-21
Dear Journal,
    I was lying in bed late last night thinking because I couldn't sleep. I was thinking what it would be like if God didn't make any people or anything. There would be nothing. I wish I wasn't made to be shy because its hard. God should've made me a little bit talkative. Anyway, I'm glad that he made a world.

My response: *One correction, my friend. God didn't make you shy and quiet. You did. So you can correct and change yourself.*

To help Melody, I asked her if she wanted to do an experiment like not bringing any pencils to school so she would have to borrow from one of her neighbors. I felt Melody needed my intervention because of her numerous entries on her shyness.

11-22
Dear Journal,
I left my pencils at home like my teacher told me to. But the person who I'm supposed to ask to borrow a pencil wasn't here in the morning so I could do my journal. So I just asked someone else and it wasn't someone I felt comfortable with. I'm almost finished with my experiment. I just have one more person to ask.

My response: *I am so proud of you!*

11-23
Dear Journal,
This is the last day for my experiment. I already asked someone if I could borrow a pencil. I'm getting used to people now, but I'm still not used to the boys yet. It feels good to be able to talk to people. I solved the problem with my Dad by giving him a kiss and saying good-bye to him as you suggested.

My response: *You have touched my heart with this. Take your time, talk to the girls until you feel comfortable, then try the boys. Boys and girls are very much alike, you know.*

1-14
Dear Journal,
I don't have anything to write. Anyway I forgot to bring my homework home.

My response: *You forgot? I guess you're getting old!*

1-16
Dear Journal,
I had a talk with my Dad about how I don't say good-bye to him. He told me what he said to my teacher but I already know. I

didn't tell him though. Now I'm not afraid to say bye to him.

My response: *How wonderful.*

3-22
Dear Journal,
I've been getting into trouble these past few days for talking. I'm already over my shyness and now that I'm starting to talk, I get in trouble for it. I am so mad. I don't know what to do. Keep talking or get shy again? I know I won't be able to get shy again so I might as well keep talking.

My response: *My dear, there's a time and place for talking. For example, let's say a man wanted a hunting gun all of his life. He finally gets his gun. He is so happy, he goes around shooting all the animals, pets and all. He needs to learn to use that gun only for hunting. Catch?*

The day finally arrived when I could do for Melody what I had dreamed of doing someday. Her final entry on her shyness read:

4-18
Dear Journal,
Yesterday I got sent out of the class for the very first time for talking. When everyone came out, they couldn't believe I got sent out. I don't know why they didn't believe it, I should be treated like everyone else. I'm no special person.

My response: *So now you are like everyone else ... maybe that was good in that they don't see you as a PERFECT person. What do you think? You are very special ... come see me if you don't know how special you are.*

Journals can also be heartbreaking. Denise's parents had gone through a divorce and she was now living with her dad and step-mom. Denise trusted me from the first day of school:

9-2
My name is Sandra Denise Bailey. I like to be called Denise. I was named after my mother, Sandra and my father Dennis. My parents are divorced. My step-mother's name is Lynn. My real mother has been divorced twice and just got married last year. I have two step-brothers, one in Kansas and one here. In Kansas my mother has a dog, here we have a bird. You're the first teacher I have told this because I don't enjoy writing or talking about it.
Denise

My response: *Thank you for sharing this with me, Denise. You sound like one brave girl. I hope you'll feel comfortable in expressing your feelings to me. I know it helps me to talk out my feelings at times. I'm glad you're here.*

9-20
Yesterday my mom and I talked. Now if you remember, I am living with my step-mom. Well, we aren't getting along. So we promised that we would spend 1 hour together alone doing something fun ... until next week Wednesday. Last night we fixed up our big bathroom. I know it's only going to last until next week but I don't want it to end.

My response: *Tell her how you feel about having this only for a week. She needs to know.*

I had a parent conference with her mother to help Denise communicate her needs. Denise sometimes asked to have lunch alone with me where she would hold on to me and weep out of total despair.

Thanks for letting me talk to you yesterday. Because sometimes I need to clean myself out and you are a good person to talk to. I just can't tell my problems to anybody. By the way, Melissa didn't know that was my real poem and she did not know how to react to it.
Denise

My response: *I know how you feel. Come to me anytime, OK? Re: your poem. Denise, your poems, I feel, can be understood by more adults than most students because they're so deep.*

The poem Denise felt Melissa had misunderstood was one Denise had written in class, "A Wall":

A Wall

We three built a wall,
We thought it would stand
Forever.
Then one of us put a hole in it
When she moved.

Now we two are drifting
And another wall is being built.
Another friend and I
Are chaining.
Locking comes next.

She followed our journal exchanges with another poem:

My Poems

My dad just doesn't
Understand my poems

Because of the words I use.
"Lock and Chain" between some friends
Don't make sense to him.
I wish
Just once,
My dad would understand my poems.

A small tiny fairy
Tricks a human man.
Flies over his head
Leaving a trail of
Dust.

Our journal exchanges continued.

My mom gave me a blank lined book for me to write my poems in. She also wrote a poem and it was a good one. It made me cry. I love writing a lot of poems already.

My response: *How wonderful that she's trying so hard to join you in your own interests. That's wonderful.*

Denise began to express her feelings through poetry. The following is her response to my comment that I get chills reading her poems:

You do? (get chills when you read my poems). My parents too! I have found out that many adults (my parents mostly) think it's scary to read my poems. Well, here is another one:

A beautiful tree
Next to a broken twig.
Comparison says the wind.

And blows away the twig.
Time and time again
Life has no meaning anymore.
Time and time again
Life has no meaning anymore.
(a newly made poem, this one. Not even one hr old.)

My response: *My dear Poet — How I love the way you*
show the beauty and joy and fragile feelings we humans feel ...

How do you like my poem???

Aloha ...
I love you
Aloha ...
Hello ...
Aloha ...
Aloha ...
Aloha ...
For now.

This kind of reminded me of you.

My response:

You remind me
Of a water lily
Rising above
The muddy, murky waters.
You remind me of
A blade of grass
Pushing itself
Above dry, caked mud.

You remind me
Of a rose
Slowly opening
Each petal
Toward the sun.
You remind me
Of all the poets
Who see beauty
In the littlest things.
I love you.
Miss K
4-26

Denise's last two entries read:

I have a poem for you.

Climb the mountain
Of love.
And take the
Chances of falling
Down.

My response: *This is the way to live. Then your life will be so rich.*

Walk the streets
of loneliness
And hope until
the end.

My final response: *You, my dear friend, are going to have a very rich life.*

The journal also became a place where children shared their secrets with me. One such secret concerned adoptions. Children who were adopted and were advised to keep this within their families, shared the secrets of their adoptions. It was here that they spoke, even as third graders, of their plans to someday seek their biological mothers. One day Julie came to me with, "I got a letter yesterday that my biological mother died." I held her and we both wept. She spoke of how her plans to seek her mother are gone and at the end of our session, she felt yes, maybe this is closure so she won't need to seek her after age 18. It was very important for Julie to share this with the class and I cautioned her that it may not remain private if she did. Her response was, "I want to. I trust them, they'll keep my secret."

I spoke to the class of Julie's request, of how Julie trusted each and every one of them, that Julie had something very private to share with them and turned the class over to Julie. She told them of being adopted, her plans to seek her biological mother and of the letter she had received the day before. The entire class was silent and tears rolled down many of our faces. Julie's story was never repeated by her classmates.

Cindy wrote of being born in Korea and of being adopted by her parents. She described wearing a pair of Korean shoes on arrival. Her entry was so powerful with such intricate images that I suggested she turn her journal entry into a book. Cindy's parents were very open about her adoption, so I knew this would be appropriate for all concerned. Cindy decided to use the third person point of view, ending with her own. The content of her illustrated book read:

A Pair of Korean Shoes
One day, a mother and father named Kenneth and Diane Matsuura decided they wanted one more child. They already had three children. They waited a whole year but Diane did not get a

child. Diane said, "We don't got a baby." So they decided to adopt one.

They applied at the adoption agency. Kenneth explained, "We would like to adopt a baby." So the person in charge let them fill out many forms. They had to fill out many more forms and had to see a lot of people.

Then finally, on June 3, 1981, the entire family went to Honolulu International Airport. They waited and waited. They saw a lady carrying a baby. It was their baby and I was that baby.

I had on a pair of Korean shoes. It was shiny and tiny. It was of silver, gold, red and blue colors. Today I am eight years old. The Korean shoes have a special place in our living room. They are on a glass case that has a Korean doll in it.

Today when I see the shoes, I feel special and happy that I'm adopted. I love my shoes and my new family. The shoes remind me that I was born in Korea.

Cindy's Dedication Page read: I dedicate this book to my birth mother in Korea. I also dedicate this book to my family in Hawai'i.

Her About the Author page read: The author, Cindy Kyung Mee Emiko Matsuura, was adopted by Kenneth and Diane Matsuura and their children Leigh Ann, Kevin, and Maile. Cindy is in the third grade. She enjoys spending time with her family.

Years later I received a high school graduation announcement from Cindy with a photo of her in beautiful, elegant Korean attire.

Donn wrote of his passion for fishing almost daily. Throughout the entire school year, Donn would walk into the classroom with an ice chest and with a knowing, private smile, would quietly put it under my desk. In it would be fish for my dinner. It was a private gift for me and we discussed his fishing and my dinners only in his journal. When he was in middle school, he called and delivered part of his catch from the weekend. In high school, Donn transferred his love for fishing to baseball and went on to play for the University of Hawai'i baseball team.

Maikel O'Hanlon, whose love for writing matched my own, privately called me Mrs. Einstein in his entries and I never disillusioned him by telling him I really was not as bright as Albert. On the last day of school, he gave me a baseball cap with Mrs. Einstein printed in gold. No one in class knew of Mrs. Einstein and Maikel. No one knew, too, of how Maikel disliked his last name because as he would say, "Can you just hear the announcer saying the quarterback Maikel O'Hanlon? It just doesn't sound right." He went on to major in English in college.

Anna used her journal to get my attention, as I often was so involved with students during the school day that it was impossible for them to even have a few minutes for a private chat unless they remained in at recess or after school, as many did.

Anna was moving out of state and asked that I continue to send her my lesson plans in writing and reading because she didn't want to miss out on anything. I promised her I would and we corresponded for a year after she left. We discussed books and Anna was continuously analyzing her own progress as one entry clearly showed:

I have been reading your letters to me in third grade and I have a feeling that my writing skills have gone down. I think it may be the trauma of running a mile every week.

The journal became an excellent place to evaluate students' writing. It would thrill me when I saw the use of the possessive apostrophe S in their entries soon after our exploration of this punctuation mark, or a reference to some of our discussions in class.

It was a place where students were told of all the good they were doing as well as a place to remind them when they were not achieving certain standards, all done with humor and lightheartedness but also with a serious pen. I felt students needed to know the specifics of their skills so that these skills would eventually come naturally.

When Philip first began writing, some of my responses read as follows:

Are you sure you're in the third grade? Are you sure you're not a sixth grader in disguise? Only yesterday did we talk about capital letters and you used capital letters at the beginning of each sentence. Fantastic, Philip!

Oh no! This kid must have left all his periods at home. Hey, bring them with you tomorrow.

The following day, Philip would have a period at the end of each of his sentences.

Hey, hey — you forgot your vowels? Where are they?

The following day I wrote: *Look at the vowels!!!!!*

One vocabulary item that brings a smile and a chuckle even today is "exceedingly." I had chastised the class in jest one day of how I was tired of the word "very" and couldn't they use words like "exceedingly." Thereafter, almost every journal entry and assignment in our Writing Workshop glared with "exceedingly." Ryan took this word to Boston College with him judging from the many writings I received from him.

The journal was also an excellent means for fostering individualized learning. Ryan was an incredible reader and writer in third grade and we both nurtured this in his journals. I could be honest with Ryan because of his subtle sense of humor and we got to know each other well through our written and verbal exchanges.

He was a challenge. One day in science class I defined the word symbiotic and the following day Ryan tossed the word right back to me when I had said no to one of his requests. "Okay, Miss K, does this mean you and I have an unsymbiotic relationship?"

Ryan was reading books beyond his designated grade level, so it was through the journal that I was able to individualize my instruction. In one entry I wrote:

> *Hey, you're a poet. You used similes. Great writers often use this technique to describe what they're writing about. Let's see whether you can find the simile that you used. This is like writing your own test, right?*

Ryan: *The simile was the eggs part. Ha! I got you there.*

My response: *Now that you are considered a great writer, how about getting rid of those "tired, overused words?" You know, like "good," "stuff" and "fun." Be thinking of other words so I know exactly what you mean. Let's have an agreement here. You can always not agree with what I'm saying — you can argue or defend your writing. But, like a lawyer, your defense must make sense.*

Ryan: *So you want to go to court. Eh?*

My response: *You have such stimulating ideas and thoughts but most of them are concealed inside you. Please ... please write in more details so I can get into your head.*

Ryan: *Right.*

My response: *STOP! Right there! Hold that pencil! You are still keeping all your ideas and feelings all locked in your head. Your responses are still "OK, yeah, yes, no." No more. I will not accept these answers anymore. You are to write in paragraphs hereafter.*

The next entry from Ryan read: *On Wednesday I got a ribbon on my Reflections letter. The theme was "If I had a Wish." My wish was to meet an alien. I had to read it so I did and mom said I was the best.*

My response: *Congratulations! I didn't know I was tutoring a winner. How did you feel when you discovered you were a big winner?*

Ryan: *I felt*
Happy
Shocked
Nervous
Excited
Surprised
Impossible to feel all these things at once, yeah?

Through the journal, Ryan and I had some meaningful book talk. I had discussed the use of symbolism in literature and Ryan wrote the following:

Dear Journal,
I read the book Dawn of Fear. *There is one thing I would like to share about the book. In the book, there was a gun and I think it was the symbol of the war so when it was buried at the end, the boy who buried it was thinking he sort of buried the war.*

My response: *I am completely impressed because I gave you a book written for 12-year-olds and you understood the symbol. Symbols are very difficult to get because they are not explained. But you got it! You are fantastic because you said the gun symbolized the war. Remember the two kinds of wars, the real one and the war game they were playing. I was wondering, do you think he also buried his childhood after the war killed his friend?*

Ryan's response was very clear to me; I was pushing the issue too much for him and he let me know it concisely and to the point: *Yes.*

Ryan and I continued his journal for another year as he went to fourth grade. Our individualized instruction made leaps and bounds as his conclusion in a book review will show:

The author also made the book so interesting that it was like a magnet and my eyes were metal.

My response: *Ryan, the last sentence on this report is magnificent. Using similes (like a magnet) and metaphors (my eyes were metal) put you in the big league of great writers. This is the kind of writing I would brag about. I'll brag, you be humble, OK? I'm borrowing this for my next teachers' workshop, with your permission, of course.*

Ryan's entries would sometimes be pages long, computer printed. We were able to delve deeper, beyond book reports and literary devices. When he lost someone very dear to him, I gave him a book. Ryan wrote:

I understood why you gave me this book. You gave it to me because it is sort of a love book. Now I can remember him with ease. I do not quite understand why you did that.

My response: *You understand my purposes exactly. Death is usually thought of or felt like the color black … sadness, loss, gloom. I wanted it to be beautiful with memories for you.*

At the end of the year, my offer to continue his journals with me received the following response:

Not unless I'm desperate.

But I was desperate. During those years, I was teaching summer session courses for teachers in language arts through the University of Hawai'i. Ryan was my one and only resource speaker. It was always amusing to see the look of astonishment on the participants' faces when young Ryan walked into the classroom after my announcement that a resource person was scheduled for the next day. Ryan spoke of the writing process from a writer's perspective, discussed literature and answered each question like a professional. Here was a youngster answering serious queries from adults and at the end of each session, a few teachers would ask Ryan for his phone number for future references. Ryan graduated with honors from high school and went on to Boston College.

As these students grew up, I was surprised to hear how many had kept their journals. After Howie and Bob had gone off to college, they both made references to their sixth-grade journals and would reproduce some of the drawings and expressions they had scribbled saying, "I can't believe I said these things to you," then adding, "I can still hear your voice saying each of the words you had written in my journal." It was because Ryan had kept his journals that I was able to lift so many passages from his writings.

It was through the journal that I got a taste of my own bitter medicine. One year a group of sixth graders asked that I, too, keep a journal as they would like to read and respond to my entries. I felt excited about writing a journal for the students and had specified a spot on the shelf for my journal. For two days, students flocked to the shelf to read my journal but on the third day, they totally ignored my journal and showed absolutely no interest. My first hurt, ego-based reaction was "You see how self-centered these kids are? They're interested only in themselves. They're not interested in me."

Then revelation hit me right between my eyes. My journal writing was not written freely and honestly from within since college. I have always kept a personal journal and there was a distinct difference between these two journals. My students saw right through me and knew I was writing for a group of students, censoring the personal, private parts of me. I did selective writing based on, "Oh no, I can't let them know this" and yet, it was to this kind of writing I had responded "boring, dull" in their journals. So my journal lasted two days, stamped with their silent, unexpressed responses: uninteresting, not worth reading.

Students, being far wiser than we credit them for, seemed to understand where I was coming from and respected this special need of mine. When Howie graduated from college, he called me long distance from Oklahoma and began with, "Now that I'm an adult, can I ask you a few questions?" and I answered each of his personal questions about my private life candidly and honestly. We are the best of friends today through e-mail. Had I not responded to him with total honesty the day he called, I'm sure he would not greet me today with Dearest Frances, my friend.

I must confess, there was one question to which I always withheld the truth and that was, "How old are you?" Jennifer, my former third grader, and herself a teacher today, sent me a birthday card two weeks ago in which she had written, "When I was eight or nine, I believed you were 100, but that would make you 115 years old today..."

One year I blatantly said "60" when asked how old I had become on my birthday, believing 60 was still eons away. The following morning, Yoko, a student from Hiroshima, whose first language was Japanese, brought in 50 carefully folded origami paper cranes, a symbol of good luck and long life. Each crane was smaller than my thumbnail. She was accompanied by her mother who bowed and apologized because Yoko was not able to finish the 61 cranes, that she had stayed up until early morning, folding cranes for her teacher's 60th birthday. In spite of Yoko's precious gift, I continue to lie about my age.

A Poet's Song

If the pen,
The tongue,
And the heart
Filled the air
With one song,
What a symphony of truth!

Frances H. Kakugawa 🍎

10 | ARTHUR T. BEAR

Arthur T. Bear was a gift that represented all the stuffed animals and pretty dolls I never had in my childhood. One day, I shared this story with Dr. Carolyn Pang, my medical internist and friend, about how poor we were growing up, how I never owned a stuffed animal or a doll and how, during my teen years, I fantasized about a cute boy who would someday win me a stuffed animal at a carnival. The carnival never came to town nor did that cute boy. On my next birthday, Dr. Pang gave me a cuddly, brown teddy bear, which I named Adam.

Adam was later renamed Arthur T. (for Theodore) Bear. Arthur T. Bear not only became a writing teacher in my class of third graders but generated so many creative juices in my students that he made the front page of our local newspaper not once but twice!

My writing program was based on the Children as Authors Program conceptualized by Dr. Violet Harada, Associate Professor, Library & Information Science at the University of Hawaiʻi and a team of school librarians and teachers in the Hawaiʻi State Department of Education. In essence, students wrote as writers do in the publishing world; they composed rough drafts, went through the editing and rewriting process, wrote their final manuscripts and had them published in book form. After publication, they held an autograph session or Authors' Tea, before releasing their books to the classroom or school library for circulation. When I had my first book of poetry published, I recall going to the public library to check the card catalog and stood there pleased as punch to see my name and book title recorded. I observed identical reactions from the students whose books were added to the card catalog in the school library.

In our classroom, we had a very ornate chair, with a high gilded back and a plush, velvet red seat, called the Author's Chair, donated by Wayne Harada, entertainment editor of *The Honolulu Advertiser* and a strong advocate of our Children as Authors Program. The Author's Chair became the reserved seat for writers who wanted class reaction or a single partner's critique on their rough drafts, or when they were ready to share their books with an audience. It was a common sight to see children sitting in this large chair surrounded by their peers acting as editors, a task they took very seriously, and they were often relentless in their constructive criticism.

Students actually loved the editing process and, when given a choice to have an individual editor or the entire class as editors, they usually opted for the latter, perhaps because they had such pride in their rough drafts and felt they had written something so significant, they wished for a larger audience — until that day when they would have a real audience at the Authors' Tea.

One day, Trebor sat in the chair and read his story about his new pet dog. This story had originally appeared in his morning journal and it was so delightful that I had suggested he turn his entry into a book. His final line said, "I love him so so so so much." One student editor suggested that perhaps he had used too many "so's" and could he perhaps use the word "very" in place of the four "so's". Trebor said, "Thank you for your suggestions, but I like it this way."

The children turned to me with a look that said, "Do something, you're the teacher."

I commented, " Treb, you're the writer. You've heard all

the suggestions made. You make your own decision." Trebor stuck by his original "so so so so much."

When we held our Authors' Tea to celebrate the books the students had written, Trebor chose to read his book. When he was finished, one student looked at the adult guests and explained, " We thought that Treb had used too many so's but he chose to go with so so so so much." He must have felt embarrassed or responsible for allowing such literary redundancy.

In the month of May, Trebor brought his book to me and said, "You know what? The kids were right. I have too many so's." He continued, "I could change it. What do you think?"

I told him, "Treb, I personally like the way it is. When you wrote this in October, it was OK for you. This shows how much you have grown as a writer. And I kind of like that so, so, so, so, but again, the decision is yours." A few days later Trebor said, "I decided to leave it alone."

Trebor taught me a great lesson. Had I edited his first draft in the traditional way, I would have deprived Trebor of discovering for himself what writing and learning are all about. Had I red-inked his sentence, it would have been revised and forgotten without involving Trebor in the process; it would have been mine alone.

When Trebor sent me an invitation to his high school graduation in Idaho, where he was graduating with honors and was the recipient of a sports scholarship, I wrote in my card to him, "I am so, so, so, so proud of you."

Having one's own work edited by others is not an easy matter, as I had to discover for myself. I had composed a poem as an introduction to our class anthology of poems written during the school year. The entire class sat around me as I sat in the Author's Chair. After my first reading, Erin bravely said, "I don't think you need that ending. I like the ending to be where you said, "I am! I am!" I noticed several heads nodding in agreement.

At this point, I behaved as Trebor had, fighting to keep every word I had written. I rebutted with, "OK. Let me read you the poem again just as I first wrote it and I'll read it again with Erin's suggestion." This time I read the original with more expression and feeling. After my two readings, the children all nodded and said, "Yes, the poem should stop at 'I am, I am.'" They came to this decision without looking at each other for support, and had raised their hands unanimously. I had over-taught them!

I balked at giving up my ending of four lines and took my poem to an adult friend and his response was, "The kids are right. You're over-talking." With some reluctance, I surrendered the last four lines to my "A Poet's Declaration:"

A Poet's Declaration

I am a star
In the Milky Way.
I am the crest
On emerald waves.
I am a dewdrop, crystal clear,
Capturing sunbeams in the morning mist.
I am that dust
On butterfly wings.
I am that song
Of a thousand strings.
I am that teardrop
You have kissed.
I am a poet!
I am! I am!
I am that rage
In the thunderstorm.
I am that image

Of a thousand forms.
I am magic on each page.
I am a poet!
I am! I am!

We have all learned to be editors of the gentlest kind, where we always respected the writer's work. There were so many times when I saw where a child's work could lead and it took all of my strength to bite my tongue and not make that child's writing mine.

Once I visited a first-grade class where I began my presentation with, "What would you say if I said inside each of you is a poet and that poet is saying, 'Let me out! Let me out!'" I began reading some poems when a student named David began creating one aloud. At this point, I stopped and wrote his poem on the board. He had shifted his point of view from first to second person a few times and his rhythm was definitely off. I read his poem aloud several times with him, hoping he would recognize the need for revision when one student offered, "It sounds all different." She recognized what I had been thinking and I wanted to help David revise, using the girl's comment, but quickly decided, *This is not the time. This is David's first poem. These children need to discover that they are poets. Forget the rhythm.*

Instead, I read to the class a variety of poems illustrating strong rhythm. Sensing they were ready, I set them free and they wrote for one-and-a-half hours, nonstop. They worried about spelling, but I told them not to fret about it at this time. A few struggled with the mechanics of writing so I sat with them and they dictated their poems to me. One boy sat for an hour and 15 minutes without moving. The last line of his poem read, "Balloons make a rainbow."

Our Writing Workshop began on the first day of school. Instead of the traditional "What I Did This Summer" they wrote "Why I Am Special," a page or two about why they are not faceless. We then used this piece of writing as an introduction to editing, using a group process. The students were introduced to the diacritical marks used in editing and they were told that whether they are in high school or became true journalists or writers, editors use these same editing symbols. I asked them first to edit for punctuation: "Do you have a period at the end of each sentence?" If not, they used the symbol to signify the lack of a period. We edited for capitalization at the beginning of their sentences and for proper nouns. This led the class into other aspects of the correct use of capitalization, punctuation and language usage. One first grader, after going through the writing process a few times asked, "If I edit my work as I write the first rough draft, can it be my final copy?" That was my goal in the entire process, to have students edit as they wrote. She was already there.

They were also shown the short biographical sketches of authors on the jacket covers of books with attention given to the third-person point of view used in describing writers.

The students rewrote their pieces before sending them to the Editor's Box. "The teacher is the final editor" was the ground rule. The importance of editing was explained to them in this way: "We do not see published books with spelling and grammatical errors in our bookshops and libraries. So will our published work be free from errors."

After the final editing, which I did working one-on-one with each writer, they finished the final copy either in pen, pencil or on the computer. Illustrations were added before they proceeded with the rest of their autobiography.

On a large chart, the entire process of writing from rough drafts to final copies appeared so students would be able to keep tabs on where they were in the process and would not need constant teacher guidance.

- Rough Drafts
- Editing
- Rewriting, Revising
- Illustrations
- Final Copies
- Cover
- Title page
- Dedication page
- About the Author with photo
- Prologue, epilogue, optional

One set of rules was established during the editing process: each writer will be respected and all final decisions for revisions will be the writer's. We avoided words such as "should" and "ought to," and instead used phrases like "I would like to suggest," etc. To this, most students would respond with, "Thank you, I'll think about your suggestions."

After the first group editing process of the first page, students were free to proceed at their own pace. They experienced the entire writing process of the first page under guidance, which prepared them to proceed on their own. Thereafter, they would be at all different stages of the writing process.

During the school year, we held monthly Authors' Teas at our school to celebrate our "published" books, and parents and the principal were invited. These books were written in social studies, science or in other subject matter areas. The school rules allowed two parties a year; this was a way for our class to have these celebration teas monthly. Each Authors' Tea was an "elegant affair" complete with cookies and tea served in fine china for the adults. The authors enjoyed juice and cookies. A few girls even wore white gloves.

On one occasion, our writing sessions were videotaped, and viewing them later, I was most pleased the teacher could not be easily found. Rather, what was seen and heard was a low hum of voices as students worked at all levels of the writing process: some were working individually on rough drafts, a few were in a one-on-one editing partnership, and one was sitting in the Author's Chair with a group of peers listening as editors. Still others were working on final copies, book covers and dedication pages. While all this activity was going on, I found myself taking dictation from Bret who had some difficulty with his mechanical writing skills. Max was sitting with his head down on his desk.

Max was a perfect example of how writers are at work even when they have their heads down on their desks. On numerous occasions I had asked Max, "How are you doing?" and his answer was often "I'm thinking." I followed this with, "Good, have your mom type out your thinking tonight." Or if I had the time, he would dictate his thoughts to me. His mother and I had an understanding that because Max was dyslexic, he could dictate his writings to her if he was not able to do so to me in class. She was often both amazed and impressed at how structured and organized his thoughts were, all ready to be written down on paper.

Max's dictated stories showed his understanding of how stories are written. Evidence of this was that he wrote complete stories with beginnings, middles and endings, along with believable plots and characters.

I would have disrupted his thoughts had I insisted all writers write with pencil in hand, casting words on paper. All writers write in their own personal ways; I seldom face a blank sheet in my own writings. My thoughts, poems or ideas are already formalized in my mind, like Max, before I take a pencil in my hand. Once again, respect for the individuality of learning styles of each student is clearly needed.

It was in this writing environment that Arthur T. Bear

made his debut. When the children came to class one morning, they found Arthur T. Bear sitting in the Author's Chair with a note attached to his tuxedo:

I am Arthur T. Bear. May I sit in this chair? Oh, and if you can guess what T. stands for, I might let you take me home for a visit.

Before the day was over, numerous notes were attached to Arthur. Many gave him permission to sit in the chair except for a few, including Gary, the special education student, who insisted that only authors were allowed in that chair. No one guessed what T. stood for.

Days following Arthur's appearance, notes and poems penned by Arthur T. began to appear attached to his lapel. Soon, complete books supposedly penned by Arthur T. began to appear. Arthur's ghostwriters were quite busy. Just when they were written and attached to Arthur was a mystery to the teacher. Arthur became a legitimate occupant of that chair.

Another mystery made its appearance. Other teddy bears began to join Arthur with notes introducing themselves. Before long there were bears of all colors, sizes and names in the classroom.

Where to house them? Chelsey, whose father was an architect with a Honolulu firm, drew up blueprints for a condominium building to house our bears. Each condo had a bear's name attached to it.

With this blueprint to guide us, a supply of empty boxes plus many recesses resulted in the construction of a condominium. Miraculously, Chelsey had provided her father with all the sizes of the bears. The local papers picked up this story and the children and the bears in their condos made the front page. Chelsey's father went to work the following day and found the article on the firm's bulletin board with a large sign: "Another successful project by ... (followed by the firm's name)."

Carol Chang, reporter with the *Sun Press*, covered the story along with a photo of the students in front of the condominium filled with its occupants. The headline of the article read: "Bears Move Into Haha'ione Condominium."

The students started by becoming Arthur T. Bear's ghostwriters. First a note appeared, asking permission for the bear to sit in the celebrated author's chair with all its velvet finery and prestige. Then little books and stories supposedly authored by Arthur himself began to appear in the room. The students wrote on his behalf so he could sit in the chair.

Arthur T. Bear ventured into other curriculum areas, being available for overnight visits to anyone who performed a humanitarian act. Journals written by Arthur would accompany him back the following morning, describing in detail his overnight visit. Arthur went to soccer practice, dined out in restaurants, had dinner in other people's homes and played many games with the host or hostess' family members. Arthur became a prolific writer of journals, stories and poems.

In late June, a follow-up article by Carol Chang once again appeared in the *Sun Press* with the original photo under this headline:

Bearshop Estate Forces Tenants to Vacate Condo

"Bearshop Estate" referred to the then very unpopular move by local landowner Bishop Estate to convert its leasehold properties to fee simple ownership at astronomical sales prices.

Excerpts from the article:

"All proper procedures were followed," a representative of the Bearshop Estate assured the press. Kakugawa, who played landlord

in the dispute, was represented by two attorneys from her class at a hearing held May 17 to decide the issue of fee-simple conversion of high-rise homes of the hairy hordes.

Through their student advocates, the fuzzy tenants argued unsuccessfully for the right to buy the land. Bearshop attorneys pointed out, "You knew it would be leasehold — why are you complaining now?"

The children quickly became politically astute as they pressed onward in the school's mock hearing room. Since two of the three judges had helped tape together the bear building, might they not be biased in favor of the lessees?

And why were Bearshop's lawyers doing everything the teacher told them to do? "Because I pay them and they work for me," replied Kakugawa.

... the judges voted in favor of the estate ... since the real landlord had others plans for the property (summer school, for example), the lease expired immediately without the option to renew, and the little box-like homes were taken down without further complaint.

And their teacher went home for the summer to her own leasehold condominium.

Students who transferred to private school the following year took Arthur T. Bear's name with them, and many teddy bears bearing his exact name appeared in their new classrooms. Arthur T. Bear had done his job well, transporting us into our inner selves, where creativity and the desire to learn waited to be tapped. 🍎

II | A 50-Year-Old Déjà Vu

When I was 10 years old, I was suspended from school for writing a description of my teacher. This teacher seldom smiled and her favorite one-liner was, "Some people's children are so d-u-m-b!" I was a fifth grader in a combination class of fifth and sixth graders. It was reading time and she gave us a writing and reading assignment while she taught the sixth graders. I finished my work, was bored, so I solved my problem by going up to the bookshelf to get a dictionary. I took it back to my desk, pretended to look for a word, and walked back to the shelf to return the book. I repeated this for a while to entertain myself. The teacher looked at me and said, "If you walk one more time, I'm going to glue you to your seat!" I wrote a note saying, "I'll glue her to her own ass," and passed it to the girl sitting in front of me. Her shoulders shook with silent laughter and she wrote "ha ha ha" on it. I continued to exchange notes with her. I wrote a very strong description of the teacher using phases like "when she smiles, she looks like the obake." (*Obake* means a very ugly and scary ghost in Japanese.) My other descriptions were less complimentary. Without my knowing it, the 15-year-old student who sat behind me quietly tattled on me. The teacher asked me to bring her my notes and, being innocent at age 10, I obeyed her instead of swallowing it.

When she read my description of her, she was so enraged she sent me to the principal's office, but before she did, she asked the entire class, "How should we punish Frances?" It is noteworthy that many of the sixth graders were 15 years old;

they had been retained in sixth grade until they could legally drop out of school after their next birthday.

"Send her to the principal and get the rubber hose," was the most popular suggestion. Since first grade, we had been told of the rubber hose the principal used to discipline students. The story was quite believable since many of the 15-year-olds were larger than the principal. The second suggestion was, "Suspend her from school for a month."

When I arrived at her office, the principal advised me, "Never ever write your true opinions and feelings on paper because this will be written evidence against you. Just think them next time. Don't write them down." To appease the teacher, she said she would suspend me for one day, following my apology to the teacher. The next morning I got up with a stomach ache and as of this writing, no one in my family knows of this suspension.

This week a special friend of mine experienced a *déjà vu* of my 50-year-old experience and here it is in the new millennium. Miki's assignment in seventh grade was to write about something that was constantly on her mind, so she described her math teacher. Her English teacher, after reading what Miki had written, had her class work in pairs, exchanging and critiquing each other's writing. Miki's partner thought Miki's description was so accurate she asked for a copy. Just as it had 50 years ago, this, too, ended up in the principal's office. Miki's paper was circulated among her peers and a copy wound up in the principal's office. The math teacher's reaction was, "This is really me," and she let it go at that. Miki's parents were informed of what Miki had written and she was asked to rewrite her assignment for her English teacher. This was followed by a letter-writing assignment. The following is Miki's written journal comment:

One of the things that was difficult for me throughout this writing process is that I had to keep on changing my topic. I couldn't stick to one thing. One was too personal, and one was kind of mean. So I ended up doing a friendly letter to my friend. It was just right, although it seemed weird that I had to keep on editing it over and over because normally, I don't edit a letter to my friends.

Teachers like Miki's would have a difficult time developing writers who write honestly, from deep within their own genuine resources.

One year I visited a first-grade class in my role as a poet. After my visit, the teacher had the children write thank-you letters to me. Their teacher, a good friend, later confessed to me the action she had taken related to one letter. Annie's original letter read:

Dear Kakhegwa,
I hate poms bcase it herts my hand. and I hate reding pom bcause it maks me desey [dizzy].
Annie

Annie's teacher felt "that was not nice" so she had Annie rewrite her letter just as Miki was asked to do. Annie's second letter read:

Dear Miss Kakugawa,
I like your pouchy vary much. Please com again.
It was vary fun.
from Annie

The first letter was, of course, the real letter. Her confession that writing poetry made her dizzy brought a smile to my face. The lesson here is clear. When we ask children to write honestly, no holds barred, we must be prepared to handle their honesty. Otherwise, our contradictory messages will confuse them, resulting in adults who censor their writing. Is it any wonder our students say they can't write, and don't write because of the fear of the consequences? I did threaten Annie's teacher with 20 lashes for trying to interfere with a child's honest response.

During the two years I led a session on poetry at two high school Curriculum Fairs, I observed a repeated scenario. A few brave students walked into the classroom when I was available and shared their poems with me and we talked about their work. Meanwhile, the doorway was crowded with students observing, checking this adult out. Slowly they began to walk in and as the session went on, moved closer and closer to me. Their message was the same: I find it difficult to show these writings to anyone because I don't want to be judged as a person.

Miki and Annie had already learned this sad lesson as I had in my own childhood. Hopefully, over time, students will rebel as I had and go beyond the initial shame and guilt that may be foisted upon them by unthinking adults.

The following excerpts are lifted from one of my journal entries:

I'm walking to Kapoho School in bare feet and am probably 10 years old. I'm passing Uyeda Store where I overhear some old folks speaking in Japanese about the Kakugawa children. They say the youngest girl (me) isn't the smart one in the family ... that all the other Kakugawa children do well except for the young girl and how she will not amount to much. I felt so hurt and ashamed. In my mind I knew then that I would someday "show them."

Years later, I received two scholarships to attend the University of Hawai'i and my picture appeared on the front page of the Hilo

Tribune Herald. *I thought of "them." Twenty-six years later,* The Honolulu Advertiser *newspaper had a full page spread on the publication of my first book of poetry and again I thought of "them."*

Years later again, when my third book of poetry was published, the villagers of Pāhoa (we had evacuated from Kapoho during the 1955 volcano eruption) held an autograph party in my honor. I was living in Honolulu then. I had to pass the village to get to my mother's house and right in the middle of the village, at the Community Center, was a large banner saying, "Congratulations, Poet."

The next evening, I attended my own autograph party. The villagers had brought trays of food and a sheet cake with the title of my new book, Golden Spike. *I read some poems and then autographed books. In the midst of all the excitement, appreciation and mostly embarrassment, I couldn't help but note the presence of "them," the villagers from Kapoho whose conversation I had overheard as a child. When I saw "them" purchasing my book, I felt strange, undefined emotions. These old-timers, unable to read or understand English, were, out of respect for books and perhaps for me as a writer, each purchasing a book, holding it with both hands and bowing to me.*

When I was in seventh grade, I fought to keep my rights as a reader. My social studies teacher found me reading a book entitled, *The Office Wife.* She took the book away from me saying, "You can't read this book. It's too advanced for you." I fought back saying, "I found this in the bookmobile. If they don't want me to read this book, they shouldn't have this in the bookmobile. I should be allowed to borrow any book in the bookmobile."

After this incident, teachers would follow me in libraries or at the bookmobile and censor the books I wanted to read. One sympathetic teacher told me my "problem" had been discussed in the faculty meeting and they were all concerned with my advanced interest in sex. The physical education teacher was asked to work with me. I felt insulted by this, somehow different and at the same time, rebellious. I continued to borrow books from the bookmobile and I still have an old photo of me, holding one of these "too advanced" books. If any of them had bothered to read *The Office Wife*, they would have discovered it was a simple story of a boss falling in love with his secretary, completely devoid of sexual scenes. This one book title had put me on the faculty meeting agenda and as a consequence, my reading was policed.

My third-grade students were initially allowed to only borrow books designated as "third-grade level" by the librarian. Once again, I managed to get such restraints removed from my students by speaking to the librarian about my views on reading abilities and interests. I know of one child who read three shelves of books about four times over because she knew she was not allowed to go beyond that level.

In retrospect, I was beginning to become the teacher and person I am today. I was determined the fear, censorship, shame, guilt and distrust I experienced would not be allowed in my classroom or in my life. Unfortunately, some things just don't change. In the '70s, I sent a letter to the administrators in the Department of Education, questioning the use of SAT test scores as the sole evaluation of children's educational progress. I also described the circumstances under which many children take these tests: guesswork, random responses, coloring in the spaces without reading, being totally uninvolved in the testing process. I also pointed out the culturally and geographically removed items found in the tests, and how test scores cannot measure true learning as we perceive it to be in the total learning process. With so much emphasis given to SAT scores, is it any wonder parents feel these test scores are life-or-death issues in their children's education? A testing coordinator from the

State Office flew in from Oʻahu to pay me a visit on the island of Hawaiʻi to stop me from pursuing my concerns. Today, I would still send this letter out with one exception: SAT test scores no longer appear on report cards as they did in the '70s.

History continues to repeat itself and so much of history is created by people. Surely we can stop some of these unsound practices from happening today. My sixth-grade teaching partner in the late 1980s, for example, dragged one of my students into my class with a loud, "You know what your dummy did?" This was a student who attended special education classes. The next day I asked for a meeting with the principal and this other teaching, requesting that we stop working as teaching partners, and that she not enter my classroom as long as there were students in my class. My request was accepted by the teacher and the principal.

We send so many messages out to our children that, over time, can be incorporated to become part of who they are. Fortunately, those who are strong and confident will be able to let the negative work for them even in a vengeful way, as I did. But many are not so fortunate. Why not send the best of messages? 🍎

12 | A GLASS ONCE FILLED EVENTUALLY EVAPORATES

Jackie was introduced to poetry writing in a sixth-grade class of mine. She became so enamored with poetry that she wrote endlessly. Sometimes she brought in her poems written on used brown paper sacks because she didn't have any other paper in the van in which she lived. Below is a sample of one of her poems:

It Hurts Me As Much As It Hurts You

As I watch my daddy drink,
I feel my heart beginning to sink.
I know it's wrong, but there's nothing
I can do and my heart turns blue.
I wish he'd stop, it hurts his lungs
But if I say something I hear a yell,
To me it would be.
I'd feel a sting on my butt, it would be.
But if he'd stop, for him it's worth it.

My heart is filled with anger.
I wish that drugs and alcohol
Had never been made.
It's a waste of money and a waste of health.
Your punishment is worse than you think.
Your loved ones are punished when you are gone.
So think before you pick up that glass
Or even that cigarette.

Have you ever watched a loved one drink?
Don't you get mad?
That's what I was thinking when I wrote
This useless poem.
I watch my father get dead drunk.
I feel like punching him in his face.
But it's his life and it's his health.
If he wants to waste, let him waste. But I,
I will not drink or smoke
Because of my loved ones.

As I write this little poem,
A tear falls from my eye
Which is sharper than a knife
Going deep into my heart.

I feel another hurt
Coming inside me.

Jackie wanted this poem published in our class anthology but because it implicated her father, I took the poem to the beach where Jackie and her family were living in a van. When I showed the poem to Jackie's father and told him how Jackie wanted it published in our class anthology, he read the poem, looked at me as I stood on the sandy beach in my high heels and said, "I guess this is the sacrifice I have to make. Jackie keeps saying she wants to be a poet just like you."

That year, Jackie wrote both poetry and narratives. When I read *King Arthur and the Knights* to the class, she wrote a story cast in a medieval setting filled with poetic medieval images. In this class we read a lot, listened to literature, and together explored, experienced and experimented with language and in the process, enjoyed ourselves immensely. This involvement with language in its totality clearly had an impact on Jackie as well as others.

When Jackie was a sophomore in high school, I made contact with her because I was curious to see how she had evolved in terms of her writing as well as in her own life. I invited her to my apartment to help her bake her first fresh apple pie to take home. When I saw samples of her poems, I felt so saddened and also angry at her teachers. She did not have access to any libraries because of a very strict and controlled family life, but what was happening in school? Her writings were as I had seen them in sixth-grade with that Hallmark-like quality. I came to the conclusion she was still tapping into her sixth grade bank of knowledge because that was all that was available to her. There had been little or no cognitive growth in terms of language and the development of her writing.

Years later when I received a wedding invitation from her containing a poem she had written, my conclusion was supported; even after graduating from high school, she was still writing like a sixth grader, unlike two other classmates of hers, Howie and Bob.

Where Howie Magner and Bob Webster are concerned, there is an almost magical aura. We went our separate ways after sixth grade since their parents were in the military. When the two were sophomores in high school in different states, I heard from both of them for the first time since our sixth-grade days together. They both mentioned journals they had written in our sixth-grade class, which they not only treasured but still read from time to time. I was delighted when they enclosed some poems to assure me they were still writing.

Bob sent the following poem, which he wrote following his grandfather's death:

Writing Is Wonderful

Writing is wonderful.
It is a thing that can make the dumb speak,
The deaf to hear, and the blind to see.
Writing can bring out true emotions
That we usually don't see,
And it brings out our true selves.
When a person writes, they can say what they want,
And no fear shall be present
That another's anger might come.
When you write, unlike spoken words,
If you write the wrong thing, you can change it
Before it could hurt someone's feelings.
Also, when you write, you can say what you want to,
And no one will tell you to shut up or to bug off.
However, most importantly,
Writing can express a person's love for another,
For sometimes, a great friendship or love
Can never be described by spoken words alone.

Robert E. Webster

Howie sent sheets of poems expressing, a teenager's world:

Thoughts

The inside of a person's head
Can be so confusing,
Full of thoughts
And feelings and opinions.
One might wonder how so many

Thoughts could survive
In such a small place.
But they do.
Would it not be amazing
If you could pick
One person to
Look into their head
And view all of the
Thoughts inside of it?
Well, here is my head,
And here are my thoughts
Spilled onto this paper.
Enjoy.

What Makes It Special?

What makes a poem
A special thing
Is not its form or style.

It's not the rhyme
Or even the rhythm.
It's the poet's trial.

When an author writes
A certain poem
He's not looking for money.

He's trying to
Write something meaningful,
Serious or funny.

He's giving you
A piece of his thoughts
Yet keeping them held tight.

He's relating a tale,
Something special to him.
Something just calls him to write.

So if you decide
To become a poet
Or even give it a whirl

Don't do it
For the money
Or try to win a girl.

Do it for
A special reason
Something deep inside.

Use a poem
To say those words
You no longer want to hide.

Howie's great sense of humor and quest for a safe future appear in the following poem:

Letter to the Editors

Dear Sirs,
Are you nuts!?!
What's the problem, guys?
Don't you realize that the

Life of every person in
The world centers around
Your decisions?
Don't you realize that I want
To get married
And have kids?
Call me selfish,
But I think that there
Are other teens
Out there who want
The same thing.
Come on, guys.
Think about us
For a change.
Think how good you'll look
In the history books when it says
That you started
World peace.

This poem of Howie's made me want to go seek out the perfect girl for him:

Too Much?

There are times when
All I want to do
Is cry.
This is because I think
I am alone.
I know I still have friends
But I want something more.
I want to be in love.
Is that too much to ask?

I think not.

The next communication from the two boys arrived when they were seniors in high school, preparing for college, then as freshmen in New York and Tulsa, Oklahoma. Surprisingly, invitations to their college graduation arrived on the same day. Bob received a BA in English and Howie received his in communications. Bob enclosed the following note:

"I don't know if I have ever really thanked you for the guidance and inspiration you have provided over the years, in my development as a student, poet and person. I don't think I would have the love of literature and the need to create and feel quite the way I do today if our paths had not crossed. Thank you for everything, my friend, and I hope to see you very soon. We have a lot of catching up to do. Love, Bob."

Howie also sent along a note with his graduation announcement:

"Every time I read one of your letters, I realize why I became a writer. While it is true that I, too, needed an escape from my pain, it was your writing and encouragement that inspired me to begin. For that, I must thank you, though I cannot repay you."

My response to former students who write and say they don't know how to repay me, is always the same: "Repay me by being happy."

Bob, Howie and I made a pact when they graduated — that we would meet in a plush bar decorated with red velvet and low lights for a reunion at a prescribed future date. Given the setting, we would need a designated driver and agreed to flip for it.

I offer the following to further enlighten the reader as to the magic that exists among the three of us. One summer, I was teaching a course in Literature and Language at the University of Hawai'i. I shared the almost kismet effect of Howie and Bob, and they became real to the teachers through their poems and letters. I recklessly said, "I'm sure Bob and Howie will write before this course is over. I truly believe this."

Three days before the course was over, I received a letter from Bob. The teachers were in awe of this special wavelength that seemed to exist among us. The next day they asked, "Did Howie write?" and I nonchalantly, if not somewhat smugly, said, "Yes" and took out Howie's letter, which had arrived the previous day.

Our relationship today is that of adult and adult. I have watched these two boys grow into intelligent, witty, kind, caring and beautiful men through their letters to me and their poetry. They have expanded and invested in their knowledge and experiences, and they continue to do so today. It is pure joy to communicate with them through friendly gibes, laughter and tears, as we remain a close part of each other's life.

For example, in one letter I had facetiously responded to Bob in this way:

I think the man has been over-educated. He should have stopped at sixth grade. Why can't he ask me questions like, "How are you? How's the weather?" No, he has to ask me about "the pen as purgation." Before I answer this, you will need to realize that I am now a very mature, experienced woman who considers herself worldly. Hence, this answer from a woman who has spent the last 20 years searching for truth in the world outside of herself and has now returned back to herself. (Ah, you think she's going to cop out). I now look at men and women in ivory towers and literature with a slight smirk and say, "Your perceptions and ideas which you hold to be truth do not fit with mine … the question is, who is right?

Basho, a haiku poet, once said, "Learn about the pine from the pine, learn about the bamboo from the bamboo." Go fill your cup.

Last year, in another example, Howie discussed with me the movie *Rounders,* relating it to his own fantasy of someday becoming the best poker player in the world:

One of my favorite aspects of the film is his relationship with a law professor. He has a great trust of the man and is quite inspired by him. And as I was watching their relationship played out, I couldn't help but draw a parallel between them and us. The law professor helps Damon follow his poker dream. You help me follow my writing dream.

No pressure, but I view you as a mentor of sorts. Not with regards to sportswriting, but with writing and life in general. Your support when I was in sixth grade made me believe that I could succeed at this craft. Your words of wisdom since then have helped me believe that I could succeed in life.

If some day I ever find a way to the World Series of Poker, I hope you can join me there. You might be out of place, wearing a designer dress instead of the common T-shirt, sipping Chardonnay as opposed to slugging down a bottle of beer, but I'm sure you'd have plenty of fun. Until then, I'll attempt to repay all the kindness and wisdom you've shown me by being happy.

This is precisely what Dr. Robert Clopton had cautioned me about when he said, "Never say you *had* this course or these courses from me." In teaching, there really is no past tense.

Many years ago I worked as a writing resource teacher, visiting various classrooms using the Writing Workshop concepts in helping students go through the entire writing process from rough drafts to final publication. Today, would I use the same techniques I used then? No, because I have learned so much more about how children best learn and I have become so much more comfortable with the writing process that I am not nearly as controlling as I was then as a writing teacher.

Three years ago I met a teacher in whose class I had worked more than 10 years previously and she related to me how grateful she was to me because she was still using the same techniques I had demonstrated in her class. In my heart I couldn't accept her compliment, but in keeping with at least a certain school of social correctness, I couldn't express my real feelings: "My dear, the contents of that glass have long evaporated, why don't you go fill it with new knowledge?"

Bob and Howie are examples of two boys who kept replenishing their glasses beyond their sixth grade year with me. Students can have more than 50 teachers during their years in school, K-12. Imagine what can be learned from 50 mentors. Imagine how their glasses can be filled, renewed, replaced with new knowledge, layer upon layer, year after year. Imagine teachers so full of passion and knowledge of their own subject areas that teaching becomes an act of creativity and art.

And finally, imagine students being in the presence of these teachers for 13 years, learning and developing many skills utilized during the rest of their lives. What a gold mine!

And yet, schools can become a gold mine only if teachers, like their students, continue to fill their own glasses of resources. Teachers can't be everything and everyone to all students. Teachers, aware of this, continue to attend training workshops and enroll in courses during their summers or after-school hours.

Teachers live, knowing how precious time is in the course of the day and how often hours spent in school leave energy for little else. Letting this lack of time affect our teaching becomes detrimental to our students. So what is a teacher to do?

Teachers, too, need mentors and resources outside of

themselves to keep their glasses filled with new advances in knowledge. Students, of course, need teachers who are knowledgeable and creative, who continuously fill their own glasses with the best of knowledge and let go of the obsolete. Can a teacher be all of this?

Three foreign students reminded me of a partnership I depended upon during the course of my entire teaching career.

Adam had come from Hungary and soon after he arrived, he stood outside our classroom with a look of total wonder on his face and said, "Do you know there's a library here with all kinds of books and I can borrow them? Do you know there are hundreds of books in there? This is such a beautiful school, not like Hungary." Adam gave me a new pair of eyes that day.

Aaron, a 16-year-old Vietnamese student said, "Do you know you can learn to play any musical instrument by going to the library? Do you know there are all kinds of books there?" And he taught himself to play the piano, clarinet, saxophone and guitar while taking flute lessons, and he mastered them all.

Kenji, who had come from Hiroshima, told his mother America was so wonderful that his teacher passed out candy in class. It was the first piece of candy he had eaten in a classroom. He took home stories of how he could call me by my name instead of the Japanese title of teacher, *Sensei*. And like Adam and Aaron, he discovered the library. He always carried a book with him, even if he couldn't read the English. To be able to walk out of the library with a book was a precious privilege to him. These boys saw our country's free and abundant of resources and discovered what the rest of us took for granted.

"Yes," I said, "the library, like the sun in our solar system, is the center of our schools." How well I remember my first impression of the librarian in the library as evident in the following journal entry:

I fell in love with the printed word when I first learned to read in first grade. It was then I had promised myself that someday I, too, would have my name on a book as author. Could this have been nurtured because certified teachers never reached our remote village of Kapoho and my teachers didn't know how to spend their time with us except to read to us? All my teachers, grades one through six, were high school graduates from nearby villages. They spent hours reading to us. I remember Homer's The Iliad and The Odyssey in fifth grade, Huckleberry Finn and Tom Sawyer in lower grades and my beloved Peter Pan somewhere in between. We had hour-long naps for six years where I once tried to pierce a friend's ears by sticking a straw from my mat through her ear lobes. She never got her ears pierced because the teacher caught my ear-piercing practice. We did gardening where we hoed the ground, planted vegetable seeds and grew vegetables, which we sold to village stores, using the money on Christmas parties. We learned to crotchet from the cafeteria manager after serving lunches and washing dishes. We had all-day May Day programs, Christmas programs at night, and parents did the waltz and foxtrot after PTA meetings.

The only books available to us were from the bookmobiles that visited Kapoho about once a month. That was as exciting as the summer days when the vendor came to sell materials for our fall homemade school dresses.

In later years, I visited the community library in Hilo and it was then I immediately changed my career choice from becoming a policewoman to a librarian. I observed one of the librarians reading a book in the back room and thought, "That's what I want to be, a librarian who reads all day long and gets paid. What a great job."

I spent my summer months sitting on the front porch, reading whatever I could get my hands on, dreaming someday I would be paid for reading. I even read Lady Chatterley's Lover and Fanny. (Censorship didn't exist on that porch.)

This love for the printed word followed me into my classroom for the rest of my career and into the lives of my students. Students'

"You love books, don't you?" also came to mean, "Then I must learn to love books, too." We all learned to be immersed in literature, so we could experience life with such enrichment, it seemed almost inconceivable to live without knowledge.

I have often compared the library to the physician's office. When ill or in need of medical help, I sought the physician; when in need of curriculum help, I sought the librarian.

The wonder of knowing how students best learn is that this understanding can be applied to any grade level or in any medium. Helping a student learn by honoring his prior knowledge, encouraging his ability to think and problem solve to make his own decisions, and respecting his passions and interests are basic to all learning. These can lead to building levels of skills, one upon the other, year after year, in each student.

The librarian can become our mentor and teacher. For example, instead of reinventing the wheel repeatedly, I partnered with the librarians to secure information for my units of study in all subject areas. Whatever I lacked in expertise and knowledge, I sought the librarians for resources. Falling into the category of dummies in technological education, I asked them to help my students go beyond my own limitations so they could use the Internet as a source of information and create their own Web sites in their educational projects. This house of resources is limitless.

I echo the discoveries made by Adam and Aaron, "Do you know there is a gold mine in the library? Do you know there is someone there who can help you with all kinds of research, information and resources? They can help you with the latest books in publication and current information available in technology. Do you know it is here that school walls, which tend to isolate us from the outside world, can be torn down? And do you know librarians do not read all day long?" ❧

13 | TEACHER, YOU'RE DOING GOOD!

I walked into the bakery, where everyone knows my name, for my weekly morning ritual: a cup of coffee and a table where I write in my journal book before going to work. This particular morning, the young woman behind the counter seemed upset and confused as she tried to serve the person in front of me. She announced the cash register was broken and she didn't know how to calculate the four-percent sales tax. I explained how to add four cents to each dollar and a penny to each quarter of a dollar. I quickly devised a makeshift chart for her, showing the pattern on how this four-percent tax is attached to every dollar and parts of a dollar. For over nine months, until a new register was purchased, my chart was pasted on the counter next to the register for daily referrals.

An elderly World War II veteran who was listening quietly to my lesson on four-percent sales taxes waited until I was done, then commented, "These damn kids, they don't learn anything in school, always fooling around." I looked straight at him and said, "I was going to say, 'These damn teachers, they're not teaching our kids.'"

We were both right in that two parties are necessary in the teaching-learning process but often, the responsibility in this process is all too often reserved for the learners only. Consider the number of tests given to students in school evaluations. Learning can take place only if teaching has occurred. The quality of this learning will be reflected in the test results.

Teacher evaluation has been the subject of countless discussions and debates among teacher unions and boards of education for years. Questions ranging from who does the evaluation to what mechanism would best show results are still unanswered in many school districts. My best evaluations came from my students. Unfortunately, there was no evaluator present to applaud my efforts and possibly recommend a raise in my pay!

My first year of teaching took place in Michigan, and in that very Midwestern setting, I was an object of curiosity. One day a minister stopped me on the sidewalk and generously offered me sponsorship. I gently explained that I was a native-born American citizen and didn't require sponsorship. I had offers to appear on television talk shows to speak about Hawai'i. I was also invited to various PTA meetings where I was faced with questions like "Do you people believe in gods?" Parents were curious and concerned about their children's "foreign" teacher. The principal visited my classroom to observe my teaching. She stopped her visitations after just one of my reading periods. I had dismissed one reading group when Linda, hugging her reading book to her chest with two hands and eyes sparkling, said loudly, "Miss Kakugawa, you really love kids, don't you?"

One April morning, my third graders were busy at their desks, working on their math. The only sound was that of the heavy rain falling outside. Jeffrey, without lifting his head, said, "Look, Miss Kakugawa, stabbing rain," and motioned his head toward the window. I felt so exalted at his observation that I disrupted the class and shared what Jeffrey had said. I had read a book to the class months ago and had discussed the author's use of "stabbing rain" to describe rain beating against the window. I compared "stabbing rain" to "it was raining hard" and pointed how the author's use of language was so powerful in creating such an image that we could feel and hear the pelting raindrops. And that we, too, could do that with language.

The students' reaction to my disruption was one of silence and a look that said, "There she goes again, one of us made her excited about learning something." Jeffrey was pleased, I knew, but he concealed his feelings by continuing to work on his math problems. That moment when Jeffrey mentioned the stabbing rain was one of those golden teachable moments teachers live for. Unfortunately, such moments, the result of the meshing of what a teacher has taught and a student has learned and applied, do not appear on evaluation sheets.

One September morning in Hawaiʻi Kai, on the first day of school, I promised Destiny and her brother Philip that I would teach them not only to read and write in my third-grade class, but to love to do both. On May 1 of that school year, I was on recess duty when Destiny approached me and said, "Miss Kakugawa, you really kept your promise to Philip and me." (The whole story is told in Chapter 7.)

What other evaluation did Philip and I need after that moment?

Teachers at all grade levels are continuously evaluated throughout the school year by their students' comments about schoolwork and their academic and social progress. Quite simply, teacher evaluation is directly related to student learning.

We cannot falsify enthusiasm, love and our commitment to teaching and learning by means of evaluation forms. Where do we begin to certify that both processes are in progress at their maximum levels in each classroom? We must begin where students are present — in the classroom. The best of buildings, textbooks and curriculum will not make the difference unless our classrooms are filled with the best of teachers, for learning is a humanistic process. This has been, and will always be, the challenge of our educational system. 🍎

Sunsets

What I learn today
Can become obsolete
Before the sun sets.
Let there be
A hundred and one sunsets
In my lifetime.
Plus more.

14 | THE MAGIC WAND

Where do all those magical, golden moments that happen between teacher and students come from? Those times that bring a great "awe-ness" to teaching? Is there a magic wand from childhood fairy tales that sprinkles fairy dust around classroom walls? Or is it teacher-created?

One day I met Maikel, a former third grader, on the sidewalk during my exercise walk. Now in high school, he shared a research project he had just handed in — a 23-page English paper on Langston Hughes, Robert Frost and Emily Dickinson. He had selected three works by each of these poets. By coincidence, they were the exact poets whose poems I had memorized a few months earlier for no reason at all. So there we stood, on the sidewalk, reciting poetry.

The act of the two of us reciting these poems together, represented one of those golden moments. I knew Maikel was experiencing similar emotions by the touch of tears in his eyes. I later captured that moment in my personal journal and sent a copy to his mother, knowing many teenagers usually answer their mothers' question "Anything special happen today?" with "No, not much."

I continue to be that great tattler to many parents. Or perhaps the sprinkler of fairy dust. This year, for example, I sent an e-mail to the mother of a former student in which he described his feelings after his dad died suddenly from a heart attack. His mother appreciated what her 30-something son was going through as he did not communicate his feelings, perhaps to protect her. Was I tattling again, or just sprinkling some fairy dust?

Ryan had gone ahead of our third-grade curriculum and his classmates knew this because of the books he was reading and the additional work he was allowed to do in class. His peers respected Ryan for who he was and what he was capable of accomplishing. They knew, "Ryan is Ryan and I am me."

Robert, another student, decided he wanted to be like Ryan. He came to me with, "Why is Ryan so smart and I'm not?" I responded, "Why don't we ask Ryan?" Ryan, after some hesitation and a look of surprise to be called smart, said, "I guess it's because I read a lot."

Robert then asked for a parent-teacher conference saying, "I want my parents to be like Ryan's. There is something my parents are doing wrong." I honored Robert's request and met with his parents. They confessed they were bogged down in their new careers and that they had been neglecting Robert. The next day, Robert walked in with a copy of the *World Almanac*. Throughout the day he would flip to a different page and ask me questions. I answered those I could and to others in all honestly said, "I don't know, what's the answer?" It delighted Robert to be told he sometimes knew more than his teacher. The *Almanac* became his constant companion for weeks, until he felt he had reached par with Ryan.

What was the source of this respect for Ryan? We were all doing something right. Ryan, in his low-key manner, was a natural and humble learner, and perhaps my obvious respect for all learners had something to do with it. Or was the combination of Robert, Ryan and myself the magical trio? If I were asked to do an encore on these happenings, I would not know how to replay them because they did not appear in any lesson plans or in any curriculum guides available to me.

Destiny came to third grade on the first day of school

and said, "I can't spell. You have to teach me how to spell." Destiny was right. She was a very poor speller and the harder she tried, the worse she became. I could see the frustration in her face and body language.

I tried to give her the message she was doing fine with her writing, even with some of her misspelled words, pointing out the reason why, in our writing process, we go from rough drafts to editing before producing the final copy. I didn't know how else to help her until I read an article in the daily newspaper about a Pulitzer Prize-winning writer. He confessed he was one of the world's worst spellers. When asked how he could be such a prolific and successful writer when he was such a poor speller, he answered, "I married a good speller."

I took the article in to Destiny and said, "Destiny, I found a solution to your spelling problems. Hereafter, forget handsome boys or boys who are rich or are good dancers. The minute you meet a nice boy, ask him, 'Are you a good speller?' and if he says 'Yes,' marry him." I gave her the article and that was the turning point in her writing life.

Like magic, as it usually is with children, Destiny's spelling began to improve, now that she had set aside her self-imposed belief of failure. For the next two years, she came to me during recess with a group of children behind her and asked, "Miss Kakugawa, isn't it true that you told me I didn't need to worry about my poor spelling because I could always marry a good speller?"

Children often came into my classroom with their own magic. My morning routine was to go to class an hour before the first bell so I could leisurely brew a pot of coffee, sit at my desk with my first cup of the day and greet all the children who were dropped off very early in the morning by working parents. One morning, I was too involved in my work to have my usual cup of coffee when I heard someone say, "Madam?" I looked up and saw Leo, one of my third graders, standing there with a white paper towel draped over his arm like a waiter. He bowed and offered me a mug of coffee on a tray with, "Your coffee, Madam." He knew by my reaction he had done just the right thing at the right moment for his teacher. Unfortunately, that had to be his first and last offer to me because for safety reasons, I carefully explained to him he could no longer bring me coffee because I didn't want him burning himself and others by handling my pot of hot coffee. But I have kept this precious gift from him tucked away in my memories all these years.

My first marriage proposal occurred during one of these magical moments. One day when I was a student teacher at the University of Hawai'i Laboratory School, I was on the playground with a class of four-year-olds when Ken came running to me holding a leaf in his hand. "Special delivery letter for you!" he shouted and handed me the leaf. I took the leaf, then returned it to him saying, "I need to watch the children, so can you read your letter to me?" He looked at his leaf and read, "Dear Teacher, I love you. Will you marry me?" I picked up another leaf from the ground and read my response, "Dear Ken, yes, I will marry you." He ran off with my leaf.

A few weeks later, Ken's father visited my classroom and after introducing himself, said, "I came to meet my future daughter-in-law. Ken speaks of nothing but you." He shared how at the dinner table Ken had announced that when he grew up he was going to marry me. His oldest brother had laughed and said, "She'll be an old lady by then." Ken's answer, angry and defiant, was, "She will never grow old."

Often, there are moments when realities overpower this magic.

One morning, six-year-old Jamie, who was fighting a battle with cancer, followed me out of the classroom after my visit as a writing resource teacher. He said, "I love to hear you talk. I love your voice. I feel I am in church when I hear you talk." How I wished then that I had some fairy dust to sprinkle over him to cure his cancer.

Jamie continued to touch me. One morning, he waited for me to share a dream he had the previous night. "I had a dream that you and I were having dinner together by candle-light. We were drinking wine and we were having a good time."

Was he given a glimpse into a future he would never experience? Or was he given a gift of seeing himself as a man, enjoying an intimate dinner with a woman? I carried this ache in my heart for a very long time. He would later tell me, "You are the most beautiful woman I know."

There are times when Mother Nature brings this magic into the classroom, by way of a child staring out the window. It was during my third year of teaching first and second graders in a school near Hilo on the island of Hawai'i when I heard a window-gazing student say, "Red ran away." Red was a first grader in my combination class of first and second graders. It was early September so this was not unusual, as children not quite adjusted to school would sometimes leave the classroom without permission, deciding home was a better place. I ran out of the classroom to look for Red and was awed by what I saw.

The entire baseball field next to our classroom was slow-ly being covered with fog. I saw Red running into the fog, his hands spread out like a soaring eagle. I stood quietly and watched him. His figure became less and less distinct as he ran and ran to the end of the field where the fog was thickest. Then he turned and slowly returned to me. There was total puzzlement and sadness on his face as he said, "I couldn't touch it. The more I ran, the more it disappeared."

I was so entranced by his remarks that I couldn't say a single word. I just put my arm around Red and we both walked slowly back to the classroom. We never spoke of the fog. But, like Red, I wanted to touch what I saw; I wanted to capture it in some form for me to keep. I wrote about that morning in my journal and eventually in a short story. Years later I tried to capture it in a poem that appeared in my fourth book of poems, *The Path of Butterflies*.

Run, Run, But Not into the Fog

A little boy
Runs into the fog
As it slowly creeps
Over the field,
Softening edges
Into mists.
He runs and runs
And soon is swallowed
By the mysterious giant.
Then slowly, quietly
He returns to me
With wooden legs
And puddled wings.
"The more I ran
The more it disappeared."

These magical moments that bring so much joy into teaching do not happen without input from teachers. Many of the moments described in this chapter could easily have passed without being noticed. Had I not memorized those poems when the unexplainable urge to do so came to me, my encounter with Maikel would have been very ordinary for both of us. Had I not created an environment of mutual respect for each of my students, Ryan would not have received this same respect from his peers nor would Robert have pursued his problems in the manner he did. Had I not picked a leaf from the ground, Ken would have experienced his first rejection of love. Destiny would perhaps still be a poor speller today, had I not taken that news article to her. And Red and I wouldn't have had that morning to treasure, had I given him a scientific lecture on fogs or reprimanded him for running out of the classroom.

This magic I speak of also lies somewhere beyond our consciousness. It is this magic, nurtured and half-created by teachers, that stops us in our daily paths to let us say, "What a privilege." These golden moments I have experienced are always there somewhere between students and teachers; we just need to recognize and spotlight each and every one of them, as they happen, to truly make them our own. And for this, we need to have our antennae up and tuned in to capture the magic. 🍎

15   Teacher, Was I Supposed To Be Dead?

Teacher, Am I Supposed To Be Dead?

I come to you with my own private self,
With baggage, if you may,
Collected over all the years
Since my birth.

Likes and dislikes, fears and delights,
Passion, too, for a number of things.
I have hopes and aspirations,
Confidence and insecurities,
Name it, Teach, I've got them all.

So here I am in your classroom
With all this baggage.
Some will eventually get in the way
Of my learning while others
May enhance my time with you.

You, teacher, will have to sort them out,
I don't even know which are which.
I guess this is why you're here,
To help me sort this baggage out.
You have the training, the knowledge, the art,
The ability to help me out.

I look around me and see all the others just like me,
All loaded down with baggage like mine,
Waiting to be sorted out.
We're all different, Teach,
Even if we look alike or celebrate
The same birthday.
If you believe one baggage
Is the same as the other,
I'm going to be in trouble,
And so will you.

Sort us out, Teach, and help us learn
With whatever good there is in each of us.
Don't give up on us by stuffing us
Into that one big mold made in your image.
(I think only someone else can do that.)

I'll let you in on a secret.
I'm not letting you in,
Until I'm sure you can be trusted.
You being a teacher, and me being your student,
Won't give you automatic trust.
No, I've met too many adults in my life,
In and out of school
And I know only a few can be trusted.

Trust comes in many shades for different people.
I know what trust is for me.
Am I going to tell you?
No, Teach, you'll have to work this out yourself.
You being a teacher, I know you'll know what to do,
How to do it, how to be the best kind of teacher I need.
We're all alive in here, just don't kill us.

Okay, I'll share one fear.
I have this one fear each time I meet a teacher,
That I'll be expected to be super obedient,
Quiet, immobile and just plain external
Without anyone taking time to know who I am.
Please remember, I'm not dead yet.

Frances H. Kakugawa

Those students who simply refused to go away after having graced my classrooms are the final echoes in this book. It took little effort to obtain their input when my e-mail to each was sent labeled Homework from Teacher. Each responded immediately.

From Ryan Hirasuna:
The best teachers don't teach at all. Instead they lead their students down the myriad paths of a soul to where each feels comfortable, until they have all found their niche. During this journey that twists and winds along that complicated highway we call life, the greatest educators among us do not simply teach, they illuminate. By bringing light into the dark corners of mathematics, English, social studies, and other unmentioned subjects, they hope to broaden horizons, increase understanding of the world around us, and ignite the fires of inspiration in the minds of the children they teach. Frances Kakugawa is such a teacher. Not only has she taught hundreds of students, she has touched the lives of many more. As I am sure the rest of this book will testify, not only is she a wonderful instructor, she is an extraordinary person.

Although the passage of time has left some memories blurred and indistinct, some stand out like shining beacons from the mists of memory. I can still recall writing that we did in that brick building which was our third-grade classroom. Every day started with "journal time," in which thirty-something students would write a page of their feelings or thoughts, in worn and battered black- and white composition books. To encourage us to be truthful, I recall Miss K (for that's what I called her then and what I continue to call her to this day) telling us to fold sensitive pages over, so she would not read them.

Oh, the thoughts that must have been hidden by those folded pages: childish squabbles with peers, troubles with homework, maybe even the first signs of puppy love. The strangest part is that I believed Miss K when she told us that she would not read these private journal entries. In a world that is so cynical and exceedingly suspicious, it's rare to find such trust in someone, especially when all it would take to find the deepest secrets of another is a flick of the wrist.

It is fortunate that I can count myself among Miss K's students. Her fingerprints are all over my life today. She has lit a fire so voracious that sometimes it threatens to consume me. It's gotten me into more trouble than I would like to remember. You see, I love to read: stories, fables, novels, fairy tales, anything that has a beginning, middle and an end. Once I start a book, it's almost impossible to put it down. I'm lost in my own world, which consists of the pages in front of me and nothing else. I read to the exclusion of the rest of the world. And it's a unique experience, to become so lost in a story that it takes people multiple tries to get my attention. Although others frequently become annoyed with what appears to be a lack of attention, I treasure this resource of mine, for how many people do you know who can escape to another world simply by opening a book?

If you are one of those people I have "annoyed" (sometimes annoyance can lead to hair pulling and screaming), I apologize, but it's all Miss K's fault. Every day along with our journals, we would have reading time. At first I started with comic books, reading the same ones over and over, until Miss K caught me and told me to read something else. Her suggestions opened up worlds of such wonder, such magic. In these worlds, heroes performed great deeds, solved impossible mysteries, and triumphed over unspeakable evil, all through the will of the author. The best part was I got to go with them. In my mind's eye, I saw the same incredible vistas, and brave new worlds the people living in the pages experienced. Because of Miss K, I discovered these worlds could be mine, just by turning a page.

It was sometime after this that I came to a shocking realization, that teachers are people. How curious it is to think that these people we see every day standing in front of a green blackboard have lives outside the classroom. I don't remember exactly when this realization found me, perhaps it was the genuine flashes of concern which glimmered in her eyes when one of my classmates took ill. Or maybe it was the way she treated her students, exactly the way she wanted to be treated. Other teachers, other grown-ups, treated us like we were small animals, deliberately slowing down their speech, and changing their vocabulary to words of two syllables or less. Miss K refused to do that. She expanded our vocabulary; in an effort to rid us of words like "very" and "da kine," she taught us words like "exceedingly," and the proper names and adjectives for so many different bits and pieces.

The brightest memory that I have of Miss K is the time she asked me to go and speak to a classroom of teachers in her University of Hawai'i-sponsored summer course. She asked me to tell them, from a student's perspective, what was effective in teaching, that I was just to tell them what I felt, and not to worry about anything else. Armed with this directive, I did just as she asked, simply writing down what I would want my teachers to do. It came out to about two pages, single-spaced on a computer, not at all that much information, but it was honest.

So there I stood, in front of a classroom of teachers, who were in school longer than I was alive, fearlessly giving them instruction on how to teach children. I looked up from my notes to see them writing it all down. Was I right? Are they going to do what I tell them? It was a sobering thought, that my words would change the lives of *others. And in the end, isn't that what teaching is about, changing the lives of others? I guess I, too, am a teacher, changing the lives of those who surround me. I only hope I can be the same kind of teacher as Frances Kakugawa.*

At the time of this writing, Ryan was a freshman at Boston College, where he went on to major in Marketing and Human Resources Management. As a third grader, Ryan often dreamed of finding a cure for Alzheimer's disease because his grandfather suffered from this affliction. He was also the photographer for my book of poems titled *Mosaic Moon: Caregiving Through Poetry*. Following is a copy of Ryan's presentation to my class of teachers in that University of Hawai'i summer course, given when he was only 11 years old.

What kinds of people make good teachers?
- *People who have a fascination for learning and are ready to share with students and with other people.*
- *People who are willing to work with children.*
- *People who like children and are patient.*

Other Bits and Pieces
- *Kids love to play games more than anything so use games to learn. If you give prizes, give consolation prizes to everyone. Your message should be: Try your best, that's all I ask.*
- *When you (Miss K) did the Nutrition Chef, that was great. I really looked forward to that every day. You pretended to have a guest lecturer and in you walked with your chef's hat, creating nutritional dishes for us to eat. You did this for a whole week.*
- *Let them know the rules on the first day. Post them on the wall so they know what's expected of them.*
- *You don't need to come in smiling and say Ha, ha, ha, but do come in with a good mood no matter how you're feeling. Your bad moods*

pass on to the kids.

Writing

- *Before revising the work yourself, ask the child, "What is your main idea? What do you want to express?" Then show the child the things that are slowing down the story. Give suggestions.*
- *Don't use "should" and don't mark the paper.*
- *Writing can be used in science and social studies*
- *There can be humor in non-fiction writing. Example: Research paper on Charles Lindbergh: "If two wrongs make a right, what can two rights make?"*
- *Let children write from their own experiences. "Stretch the truth" to add interest to everyday occurrences.*

Editing/Conferencing

- *Students prefer peers especially if they don't get along with the teacher. They'll figure out if both the teacher and the peers say the same thing.*

Reading

- *Basals are boring. Read to them chapter books, have them read books at their level and interest.*
- *Just let them read. If you teach the parts of the set they'll only look for them and won't enjoy reading.*
- *Don't give worksheets and workbooks or reading comprehension questions.*
- *Stay away from forms. Forms don't allow freedom.*
  Do reading logs. When a log is not great, don't say, "Try harder." Say, "This book doesn't sound good to me. I won't read it myself."
- *To any improvement seen, say so. Make the students feel good. Let them feel and write how they feel or how they see the story to be (own voice).*
- *Don't mark the paper. Let the students mark their own.*

*- Book-it. Don't assign a number of books for all students. Check the
students out. For a week, let them read and see how many books
are being read. Increase the numbers as they read.*

Here are some questions from the teachers to Ryan, and his
responses:

1. Why are you such a good writer?
*Because I read. I read good, hard books. I can also speak well because
of the vocabulary in these books.*

2. Do you need to know every word in the story to understand
the book?
*No, I can use context clues. Understanding the words in the book and
what the book means are not the same thing. There's a difference in
reciting, memorizing what's in a book, and telling you what it
means. Some people can tell you the parts of a whole book and not
miss a detail but ask them a comprehension question and they'll turn
blank.*

From Howard Magner:
*She is Fran to me today. Not Ms. Kakugawa or Teacher or
that old battle axe who gave me homework. Just Fran and, in turn,
friend. How this happened, I'm not completely sure. Surely the seeds
were planted with those gifts of candy in her sixth-grade classroom at
Nimitz Elementary, handed out whenever she shot a round of golf
under 100. Of course, her short game being what it was back then,
those gifts were rare, but my good friend Bob Webster and I found a
way around that. Basically, we'd accost her after school until she
relented with a Tootsie Roll or butterscotch, or even both if she was in
a particularly good mood. And since the school was but a short walk
from home, we'd even visit for a sugar fix after heading off to the
brave new world of middle school. Looking back, it's a wonder Bob*

and I weren't barred from school grounds, or for that matter, that we have any teeth left.

I maintained occasional contact with Fran after leaving Hawai'i around the age of 15, perhaps sending a letter every year or so. Figured it was only fair after all the money she'd blown on candy, regardless of how rare it was for high-schoolers to even remember who their sixth-grade teachers were, much less write to them. But it wasn't until I'd made it to the real world that I got serious about staying in touch.

It was one of those moments when you sit down and take stock of your life, wondering how you got where you were, who helped you along the way, things like that. I'd been a sportswriter for a couple of years and, despite paychecks that made waiters wealthy by comparison, I love my job. Here was a guy who'd been a sports nut since childhood actually getting paid to watch ballgames. But just as important, I was actually getting paid to write. The more I thought about it, the more I realized it was a direct result of that old battle axe back in sixth grade.

OK, we never actually called her battle axe. Honestly, she was too nice for that. I don't ever remember Fran raising her voice, which is saying something when you consider how seriously I took my role as class clown. She did, however, have something I recall only as The Evil Eye, which always signaled the end of the circus. It was one of her more memorable qualities, but even The Eye, regardless of how effective it was, doesn't rank at the top of the list. No, that honor is reserved for Fran's ability to encourage and instill self-esteem in her students to an extent that I've not since encountered.

I still don't know exactly how she did it; I only remember that she did. Somehow she persuaded a sixth-grade boy who wasn't exactly the most confident fellow that he not only could write, but that he had a gift to write. She mixed equal amounts of praise and guidance, the net effect being that I truly believed I knew the secret of stringing words into sentences and, eventually, into meaning. In the process, she *introduced me to this amazing invention called poetry, coaxing from me nothing more than basic stanzas of childhood feelings and convincing me they were on par with Longfellow, or at least a pre-teen version of him. Today, other people have therapists, while I have my poetry.*

I'm sure I learned other things during those nine months in her classroom, but those subjects are now locked in my subconscious or lost via amnesia to history. Whatever they were and wherever they reside doesn't really matter, though. The truly important lesson, the one that made me a writer, is impossible to forget. You simply don't forget those first steps along your life's path.

The funny thing is, in the time since Fran was paid to teach me, she's taught me so much more. Through the miracle of electronic mail (I'm simply too lazy to use the old-fashioned version), she and I have maintained regular contact. It's been at least 16 years since we've seen each other in person, but we know each other better than ever. She has stood by me through difficulties of family, of career, of love and of life, offering that familiar encouragement along with a seemingly endless stream of wisdom. I try to reciprocate, but do so under no illusions. She's had decades to accumulate such wisdom, a nice trick for somebody who has the world convinced she's 39, and for me to think I could match it in half that time would be arrogantly foolish. Still, whenever she has a question that's tailor-made for a 30-year-old bachelor sports writer, such as the University of Hawai'i's chances to make the NCAA basketball tournament, I'm there for her.

None of this was foreseeable during those days in her classroom, days largely spent wondering how to separate the teacher from another piece of candy, which is probably how it should be. I've always thought life would be a bit boring if you always knew what the next scene held. At the risk of challenging that premise, though, Fran and I have this ambiguous plan to someday share a glass of wine, not across the Internet, but across a table. I figure I'll bring a Merlot. Hear it goes good with butterscotch.

Howard is a sportswriter today for the *Battle Creek Enquirer* in Michigan. He is newly wedded to Nicole, and he continues to touch me deeply with his introspective, compassionate and very humorous e-mail messages. I have his promise that he will dedicate his first best seller to his sixth-grade teacher.

From Robert Webster, Jr.:

It was September 1982 when I met Frances Kakugawa, or "Miss K," as many of us called her. It was the year that I entered the sixth grade and even today I can recall how I was filled with dread at the thought of returning to school that fall. Although I had loved school in my youth (oh, so old and wise at the age of 10!), the previous year had been a difficult one. For the first time in my short academic career, I was not looking forward to the start of the school year.

How lucky I was, then, to be blessed with Frances as my teacher! I remember her enthusiasm, telling us we were going to have a great year, one that promised to be full of fun! Now, nearly two decades removed from that classroom, I can still recall the excitement I felt at the end of that first day of class. I was so full of joy, I rushed home to tell my mom and dad that school was great and the teacher was nice and she smiled a lot and she said we were going to learn haiku! It was the beginning of one of my most memorable years in school, the one where I truly developed my love of the English language and first aspired to be a writer.

Each day of that year began with time for our journals. Frances would review the journals each night and place her comments in them, following up on a train of thought or pursuing an idea she felt had promise. I always looked forward to getting my journal back in the morning, knowing there was a message (and maybe a smiley face!) inside just for me from my favorite teacher.

At the time, my mother was returning to work and I was upset at not having her waiting at home for me when I got out of school. It was something that I wrote about in my journal often and the reassuring answers I received from Frances were extremely comforting. She didn't dismiss my feelings, but instead provided me with a sympathetic ear as I came to terms with this new phase in my life.

Our journals also served as a starting point for the poetry that we would develop throughout the year. When confronted with a frustrated cry of, "I don't know what to write about," Frances would reply, "Write about the things you would put in your journal." No topic was unworthy of having a poem constructed in its honor, with my friends and classmates creating odes to birds, baseball, Atari and surfing, as well as more somber pieces about divorce and the pain of losing a loved one.

Towards the end of the year, Frances gathered our best work into a single, bound volume featuring student-created artwork to complement many of the poems. We were published poets! When that volume arrived in our classroom and we each received our very own copy, it was an unbelievable feeling. I was so proud of that book — I made sure to take it out whenever my relatives came to visit, reading over their shoulder to ensure they were giving my creations the attention they deserved.

Those exercises ingrained in me that nothing was more powerful than putting pen to paper and writing. I had always loved reading, disappearing into fantasy worlds laid out for me by my favorite authors. It was Frances who convinced me that I could do the same; that I could take my thoughts and feelings and provide them with the permanence of the printed word. She taught me that the ability to harness the English language in order to communicate and share with others was priceless — she inspired me to pursue my love of writing.

Now, that being said, there were other moments from that year that I recall fondly — moments that don't necessarily translate into the traditional "Frances, this is your life" remembrances. For example, to this day, if I should happen to stumble across an episode *of* Remington Steele *on TV, I will surely stop and watch it — if only because I am reminded of Frances' swooning over Pierce Brosnan in the title role.*

I also recall a friend of mine, Howard, and I taking care of small chores around the classroom after school for coveted "brownie points," which could be redeemed for candy. Of course, this led to the incident when, after we reattached a paper to the bulletin board, we were informed by Frances that all good deeds shouldn't be done simply for brownie points. To which Howard replied, as he removed the paper from the board, "No brownie points? No service!" I recall the weeks following that incident as being distinctly candy-free.

And I also remember when, at the end of the year, Frances presented me with a book of her poetry, A Path of Butterflies, *for having read the greatest number of books in the class from September to May. My first book of poetry, it has traveled with me from Hawai'i to New York to South Dakota and back again to New York. It currently sits on a bookcase in my and Erica's living room, safe between a copy of Emily Dickinson's collected works and a book of poetry by Naomi Long Madgett. It remains one of my favorite works to return to, whether to retrace a familiar verse or simply to look at the dust jacket photo and remember my teacher, my friend.*

Inside the book, Frances inscribed the following: "To Bob, for having read 54 books from Sept. to May. How I will miss your touch of humor. Continue your love for the printed page. Love always, Frances Kakugawa, your sixth-grade teacher. June 1983."

I have, my friend. Thanks to you, I have.

Bob is in communications at St. Peter's Health Care Services in Albany, New York. He is married to Erica Higgins. During his "before Erica years" he was not one to communicate, so it was common practice for me to "tattle" to his parents in New York about his uncommunicative ways and even to suggest that they rent his room out when he was away in college. With

Erica and a newly born son next to him now, there is no need for my subtle threats.

From Trebor Struble:
My memories of teachers and classmates don't really begin until third grade. It was in third grade when I met a person who would change my outlook on school and teachers. Miss Kakugawa presented herself as a person that cared about the extra things outside of class. She valued the time these students of hers put forth to learn the basics of her class. She recognized every student and tried to do all she could to establish a level that was near to the student and make the curriculum interesting rather than intimidating.

Well, when I was just a little guy, my first day of third grade was pivotal. This marked the point at which I was halfway through my elementary education. My mom dropped me off at school, and with my new neon clothes, which were cool at the time, I set out to class to meet a person I would never forget, Miss Kakugawa.

After the first few days of class and getting to know my class-mates, I recall that we jumped straight into poems and especially haiku. I will never forget my experience with these simple little poems. Miss Kakugawa took the haiku to a whole new level. Did I mention it was very apparent that English was Miss K's favorite subject? Well, although it was her forte, it wasn't exactly peaches and cream for me. This known fact could have been a big speed bump to my education in any other third-grade class, but Miss K's determina-tion changed my whole outlook.

I recall a specific time when the class was supposed to write some nature haiku poems and to pick one and rewrite it nicely and put it on this mini three-page paper thing. Well, while every other student cheered with joy and diligently got to work, I started out and quickly realized that all I had worried about in my life up until then involved Nintendo. I hadn't spent more than two seconds in nature; the only glimpse I got was looking out my window waiting for the next level of my Nintendo games to load. Anyway, this little assignment wasn't all that easy for me. Somewhere along the line, Miss K noticed my frustration and sat down to help me. The poem was something about a rabbit hopping in the woods and I had always thought that all poems had to rhyme. Miss Kakugawa was quick to explain that poems can come in any form; whatever anyone has to say about life is enough requirements for a poem. With this simple thought in my mind and a little push, I finished that nature haiku and took it to my parents that night to show them I was aware of more than just Nintendo. Miss Kakugawa did this kind of thing throughout the whole year.

She took issues that kids were struggling with and answered them in perspectives that the kids could relate to, rather than the normal dry straightforward answer. I am in college, and still to this day I have teachers answering my questions with the same material I originally did not understand. All of what I gathered from the classroom from Miss Kakugawa just came easy because she presented it in ways third graders could relate to.

The fact that Miss K was always thinking of ways to relate to us students enabled her to quickly establish a role in which she played an older friend and mentor. She definitely was different in that she never tried to abuse her position as a teacher and try to intimidate the class with her knowledge. To me, she just put out this vibe that she was very approachable. No matter what the subject, she seemed like she was always interested in what everyone had to say. For me, she put a different aspect into learning.

Now I don't know if Miss Kakugawa remembers this, but this is one of those memories that I will always remember about Miss K. The details are a little fuzzy, but I was beginning my interest in girls during my third-grade year. I mean this was the stage in which they started to lose the cooties and no longer deserved the harsh harassment. Of course, I had this little crush on this girl in the class, and I couldn't admit this to any of my friends because then

I would no longer be macho and might develop some cooties of my own. This was the first real girl situation I had in my life and I wasn't about to go through it by myself. I didn't want to tell my friends and I definitely couldn't talk to my parents. All I could think of was to ask Miss K. I figured she was in third grade once, and she knows the girl; she could probably talk to me about how to tell this girl that I liked her.

I stayed after class one day to talk to her about my situation, and once again she was excited and interested to give me some advice. Now I don't know what I said to that girl or even if she is cute anymore, but I do know that Miss K was always willing to help in and outside of the class. To this day I have never met a teacher that I would approach with a personal problem like that. Granted, it was a little third-grade crush, but the point I am trying to make is that Miss K never presented herself as intimidating and unapproachable. She seemed to know everything, and if she didn't, she would do some research until she did. She always tried to do all she could; she's a very nice lady.

These are just a few stories out of the whole year. The collection of events like this made my third grade year one to remember. Through my whole elementary education I think I remember two of my teachers' names, my sixth grade teacher and Miss Kakugawa. Of all the teachers I have had, Miss K is the only one I have kept in contact with. Her teaching style in the classroom made learning easier and fun for me; she made me want to come to school because seeing her was like having another friend who would be there with me. People like Miss Kakugawa are the reason that I valued going to school so much. Of the teachers I remember, the reason I remember them is because they were harder than normal or so boring that you dreaded going to class. Miss Kakugawa was different than a lot of these types of teachers. There is only one person that someone can consider his favorite, and for me the choice is easy. It is Miss Kakugawa.

Trebor wrote this when he was a freshman at Willamette University on a sports scholarship. I still recall his first sentence to me: "My name is Trebor. That's Robert, my Dad's name spelled backwards." He played on the football team and went on to major in Exercise Science/Sports Medicine at Willamette, with a math minor.

From Destiny St. Laurent:

Wow! I've finished college and I'm still getting homework from my third-grade teacher. Surprisingly, as I sat typing this out, I had no problems doing so. Ms. Kakugawa's class was one of the few classes where I actually remember a lot of things. Now the problem is, figuring out which things to write.

Ms. Kakugawa gave me an appreciation for writing, whether it be haiku, poetry, stories, even reports, all of it. The written word became an amazing thing to me. Hey, I wouldn't have become an English major in college if I hadn't been in her class, who knows where I would be now if it weren't for her.

I remember her fascination with witches, not just dressing as one for Halloween, but reading Roald Dahl's The Witches *to us. I watched the movie a few years later and it reminded me of Ms. Kakugawa. All I have to say is Angelica Huston's got nothing on Ms. Kakugawa. I recall she had on a prosthetic nose with a huge wart just above her left nostril. It really added to the authenticity of her reading.*

I also remember a Christmas house covered with Hershey kisses all over the walls and roof and we had to answer questions to get a "kiss." Oh, the best was when she was teaching us about the solar system. She had one of the students take our red rubber dodge ball and walk around another student holding a volleyball … it was supposed to be the moon rotating around the earth. Then both students walked around another student who was the sun. The funny thing about this is, three years ago I took a college astronomy course and I remembered Ms. Kakugawa's depiction of the solar system. It brought a smile to my face right in the middle of the lecture. If you really think about it, how often is it that something you learned when you were 8 or 9 would not only be remembered, but affect your life when you're 21?

It's interesting that a lot of what I'm remembering now, I have been remembering long before I got this homework. Something or someone would trigger a memory and I would smirk or smile.

I still keep in touch with some of the other kids from my class, and we all pretty much remember the same things: Ms. Kakugawa was a crazy (in a good way), eccentric, exciting, interesting and thought-provoking teacher. I was lucky to have had her as a teacher and I thank her for inspiring me.

Destiny graduated from the University of Hawai'i, with a major in English and is presently employed in the college's Sports Marketing Department. She also freelances as an editor. This is the same Destiny who believed she couldn't spell in the chapter titled "Arthur T. Bear" and was advised to marry a good speller.

From Teresa Ainsworth Todd:

It was fall in Jackson, Michigan, and I was entering first grade, wearing dresses and tights (no pants for girls), and I had a beautiful, young teacher from Hawai'i. She was so nice, patient and pretty, and she spoke with a very soft voice. Being pretty was important for a teacher. Girls could imagine being just like them someday, while all the boys fell in love with a beautiful teacher.

Our classroom was special also. It had a folding wall, and on the other side of the wall was another young teacher from Hawai'i. These two teachers, who were friends, would often open the wall for a joint arts-and-crafts lesson. These lessons were especially fun, as talking was allowed, and there were twice as many children to talk to when the wall was opened up. One craft I remember specifically was making Christmas stars from long strips of paper. We folded and twisted the paper to make a three-dimensional star, probably some type of origami. Once completed, we dipped it in hot paraffin and sprinkled glitter on them. Only the teacher could dip the stars in the paraffin, reminding us to take caution with the hot tin can. I can still recall the smell of that hot wax, and the smell always makes me think of folded paper stars. My mother still hangs these stars on her Christmas tree today.

My mother voiced no concerns to me about having a young teacher. As a matter of fact, I remember she was pleased to have some "new blood" in the school. Mom was quite young herself, well-educated and an artist. The creativity and broadening of horizons that the new teachers brought were welcoming to her, and a relief in a rather traditional rural community. It was probably my mother's respect for my teacher that kept me writing to her while I was a child, when children naturally would forget such tasks.

Because my teacher was special, I was also special. My class sang new songs that other children did not know, like "Mele Kalikimaka," the Hawaiian Christmas song. It was almost like learning a new language. We sang it with such energy, and felt smug when others did not know the words. We learned how to dance the hula and the meaning of the hand signs. We sang Japanese songs and I was chosen to wear a kimono. I wore it with my precious red patent leather shoes, as it had a big red bow in the back. We did a performance on the school stage, showing off our new Hawaiian talents. Our class was special. I was special to be in that class.

We learned to eat with chopsticks. I remember telling my mother in our kitchen one school morning, "Mom! I need to take something in our lunch today that we can eat with chopsticks!" She thought out loud, "You'll need something that's easy to pick up but won't make a big mess if it spills." My mother made me some popcorn that morning, so I could try out my chopstick talents. She let me take a big bag to *school so that others could try too, in case their mothers hadn't thought of popping corn at seven in the morning. (Thanks, Mom.)*

We did "normal" first grade activities also. We had different groups of children that had reading together, or arithmetic. We also had individual activities. I remember sitting at a round table for our reading time. This was always a special time as you received individual attention, and you were allowed to sit close to the teacher. On the first day of school, we were all handed hard-covered books instead of the usual paper activity. The book had pictures and words in it. The teacher announced that we were now ready to learn to read, and this was our first book.

As stereotypical as it sounds today, this was a Dick and Jane reader. There was a picture of Dick, along with the word. The teacher reminded us of how we use the letter sounds together to make the word. Then we began to read the book. It was fun, easy and very exciting to read! The image of that first day reading is imprinted in my mind as the exact moment I learned to read. I simply began to read. I wanted to continue reading after our table time was over (and knowing me, I probably did what I wanted to do, whether allowed to or not.) I remember going home that night and announcing at the dinner table, "I learned to read today." "Oh?" said my parents with raised eyebrows, obviously doubtful that it could be such an on-off experience. "Yes," I said, "so now I can read anything." And my confident, tiny self, believing I could read anything, went on to read and read and read.

I have read many, many things over the course of my life. In college I earned a Bachelor of Architecture, still an uncommon degree for a woman when I graduated. I am raising four children of my own and am a self-employed architect, and I'm active in church life. I cannot help but credit some of this success to a wonderful, beautiful, creative and positive teacher in my first grade class, at a little brick schoolhouse in the countryside of Michigan. Thank you, Frances.

Teresa has kept in touch with me throughout all these years with a Christmas letter. Her yearly photos show the journey her life has taken, including a husband and four sons. Just as I saw Teresa grow up from afar, I am now watching her own sons grow into adulthood.

From Jennifer Hee:
To a third grader, certain things are true.
One, teachers never lie.
Two, witches are not real — right?
I didn't know what to think when Miss Kakugawa read to my class The Witches *by Roald Dahl. In the world she read of, witches as real women gave children poisoned candy that would turn us rascals into rodents, in order to resolve the witches' hatred for children. Although storytelling is a standard part of third grade curricula, she finished the book without the disclaimer — "you know this was just a story" — and proceeded to pass out suspiciously yellow butterscotch candies. The nightmarish confusion surrounding the possibility — that Miss Kakugawa's teaching conveniently gave her access to trusting children who she'd prefer as mice — lingers with me 12 years later.*
I never ate the candy.

"I bet the 'H' in your name stands for HORRIBLE. Frances HORRIBLE Kakugawa."
—From my third grade journal

Did Miss Kakugawa pick up on my obvious brilliance from journal entries such as these? She probably didn't know then how I would succeed academically, but she did know that making a child feel exceptional was necessary for the child's intellect and, more important, personal development. Besides responding to even the most frivolous (and mean) journal entries, she wrote me notes on blue rose half-sheets to tell me I was doing well, or even just to tell me she liked me. I felt noticed in a class of 30—I felt that what I did in class actually mattered to her. I kept every note she wrote to me.

I've been hearing it all my life. My dad, telling me, "You know, you only (insert accomplishment here) because of Miss Kakugawa." For the most part, I believe him. I probably won poetry contests because Miss Kakugawa encouraged me to write about everything. But when my dad determined that the reason I was accepted into Harvard was because of my third grade teacher, I had to wonder just how much influence she has had on my academic success.

No one I know has kept in touch with any of their elementary school teachers, yet Miss Kakugawa has been a mentor and teacher to me from the age of eight until the day I graduated from college. I became accustomed to hearing her supportive, kind voice in the third grade, and I needed this voice in the seventh grade, when I struggled with a change from public to private school. I needed her voice when I was frustrated with my parents, approximately ages 13 to 20. I needed her pride in me when I won awards. I needed her to find it amusing when I tried to pierce my tongue. No matter what I did, she told me I was a good kid. Teenagers require that support—especially shy, quiet ones who have learned to write instead of just saying what they need to.

Today, I know one thing to be true. Miss Kakugawa indirectly taught me the model of the child-adult relationship that has made me prioritize the role of mentoring in my life. Having an adult consistently and subtly teach me life's lessons, by having me reflect on the experiences I wrote about from a very young age on, nurtured a desire within me to do as she has done. I want to give other children the empathetic ear Miss Kakugawa gave me during the most anger-filled and confusing period of my life. In college, I became a mentor for an at-risk seventh-grade girl, and today I work with severely emotionally disturbed teenage girls who have been abused, neglected and forced to be raised within the system. I also counsel mostly young women at Planned Parenthood on issues such as birth control, pregnancy and abortion. Quite simply, what makes me happy is to listen and write. Sincere listening, the kind that Miss Kakugawa taught me, empowers children to feel understood and outstanding.

Thanks to her, I'm convinced that the only moment I'll feel truly successful will be when I write a best-selling collection of feminist poetry — in Latin. Thanks, Miss Kakugawa! I actually believe I could.

Jennifer received her BA in Psychology from Harvard in three years, during which she sent me handwritten letters. As part of her graduation gift, I returned these letters to her in a flowered wooden box labeled "Letters from Harvard." Today, she is teaching seventh and eighth graders English and plans to go to graduate school for a degree in poetry.

Soon after the terrorist attacks on September 11, 2001, I received letters from many of my former students, each bearing a similar message: "Just getting in touch to thank you for all the help you have given me and for making a difference in my life." Jennifer sent the following poem.

Classroom Study

God help me forget what I learned
In those Ivy halls.
I was happy before
I knew how to spell Patriarchy.
I lived it, hating every ounce of me,
Hating my father saying:
"That's just the way it is."
You, being a girl, being objectified
Being worthless, moody, neurotic,

Hating my father asking:
"What's a patriarchy?"

I have no words to explain
What I cannot unlearn:
Genital mutilation
Premenstrual Dysphoric Disorder
Old Boys' Clubs
In those halls.

I should tell the girl
Whose every high school report card stated:
"She's bright but mute!"
Congratulations,
You've won the award
For spending your entire
Adolescence in a classroom.

Farther yet, I am a third grader
In an overcrowded room.
I haven't decided to talk, yet, but
Enough words flow from my fingers
That my poet teacher
Writes me letters:
"You are wonderful."
And every year since then, in letters:
"You are wonderful."

Jennifer Hee
October 2001

The messages from these students are unequivocal. The classroom needs to be a safe, fun and meaningful place for each and every student, where each student feels a personal and professional affiliation with the teacher. The need to feel special, to be respected by and genuinely cared for by the teacher comes through in each of these memoirs. Their educational and career pursuits show that learning must also take place. A classroom based solely on social relationships devoid of academic learning is one which shortchanges students. The element of creativity is crucial where the curriculum is not one based solely on teachers' guides or lesson plans, but rather is tailored to students' needs and interests. Respect for creativity in both the teaching and learning process must be present.

I was but one teacher, and there were hundreds of students. Each took from my classroom what was important to him or her. How could one teacher meet all of these needs? These students confirm what I have tried to convey in every chapter of this book — that whatever we say and do in the classroom makes a great difference in each student. This leaves no room for careless, uncaring, insensitive, irresponsible and incompetent adults in the classroom. After all, we were once the only ones allowed to wear red nail polish with dignity and honor. 🍎

ABOUT THE AUTHOR

Educator and poet Frances H. Kakugawa taught for many years in the Michigan and Hawai'i public school systems. She conducted language arts workshops for teachers in Micronesia and in Hawai'i, where she was also a curriculum writer and teacher trainer for the University of Hawai'i and the State Department of Education. In 2002 she was recognized in the book *Living Legacy: Outstanding Women of the 20th Century in Hawai'i*. She now resides in Honolulu.